BUILD YOU FOR LIFE

BY SANDY OHLMAN

Copyright © 2025 by Sandy Ohlman

All rights reserved. No part of this book may be reproduced, stored in a retrieval system, or transmitted in any form or by any means—electronic, mechanical, photocopying, recording, or otherwise—without prior written permission of the author, except for brief quotations used in reviews or critical articles.

This book is a work of non-fiction. While the author has made every effort to ensure accuracy, this book is not intended as professional, legal, or medical advice. Readers are encouraged to seek appropriate guidance for their own circumstances. The author and publisher disclaim liability for any actions taken as a result of reading this book.

ISBN: 9798993012803

Cover Design: micahplaisierdesign.com
Published by: Sandra Ohlman

© Sandy Ohlman

Sandyohlman.com

build.you.for.life@gmail.com

Table of Contents

How to Use This Book 6

Out of the Ashes   10

What's the Magic Word   21

The Wonder of Words 35

Exploring the Magic   49

The Real Magic   68

Addressing the Deep   80

Humble 85

Agreement with God   99

Grateful 116

Gratitude for the Win   125

Noble   136

The Call to Nobility   146

Saints - Old and New   154

Faithful 170

The Nature of Faith   180

Growing Faith   192

From Ashes to Beauty 205

Build You for Life 215

About the Author 227

To my husband, who told me 25 years ago, "You need to write a book." It took longer than we both expected, but I have no regrets. The story we have written privately is infinitely more important.

To my kids, you are my greatest treasure. Thank you for the grace to become a better rendition of myself. My deepest longing in life is to pour my life into yours, to help build your life, and to echo every word from God.

To my mother, who taught me that when life is messy, if we are brave, we will endure; if we are humble, we will hear the voice of God; and when we hear His voice, the storm within us will become a place of peace. No, she didn't say it like that. But with the best strength she could muster, she lived it. I follow her brave footsteps and continue the climb.

How to Use This Book

Begin with openness, not referring to the pages but to your heart and mind. Choose Openness. This book is all about discovery and strength and what happens when we commit to the process of growth. It's a building guide, beginning at the core level. In order to grow, we need coaches, people who have been where we want to go. Even if my story is radically different from yours, allow it to bring insight for your growth and strength. Openness is the key. No matter where we are on the journey, there is more to learn and much more to enjoy. Openness is more than a mental decision; it's a spiritual posture.

Building a life requires discipline to manage multiple areas of our being. Our spirit is the invisible foundation and the epicenter of power; the body and soul make up the frame, encasement, security, electrical, and plumbing. As we begin, commit to openness. Whether you are just getting started in the building process or have been building for decades, stay open, my friend.

A powerful practice for openness begins with locating yourself. You are one person on this great planet. Life is a gift, from the womb to the tomb. Take time each morning to be quiet and locate yourself in that divine gift. The next practice to position yourself as a student and explorer is to acknowledge the person and presence of God. If that's new to you, start small and allow your understanding to stay open.

I have coached hundreds of people over the past decade who were facing a life crisis and needed a plan. A typical coaching session includes a challenge to look beyond what is past and what is known and imagine the future with courage and wisdom. We have to be willing to acknowledge that life is bigger than our perspective before we can grow. This is what openness means — being willing and humble to see what you've never seen. The biggest zone of wonder for the perspective to explore involves our spiritual being and the person of God.

There is a God, and He loves you and went to great lengths to bring that love to you. He wants you to know that love and live in its light. Take the first step of openness each day in prayer and reading the Bible. If you are brand new to it, start with the book of John. Read it a few times over the next week.

The best way to use this book is with a pen in hand—ready to express your thoughts and feelings as you move through each chapter. Think of it as a springboard for your journey. Journaling is a powerful tool for discovering what you truly think and feel. Putting emotions into words is like exercise for the brain. It sharpens your mind, deepens your understanding, and helps to unpack what's still hidden inside.

When you review what you've written, you may notice some thoughts feel complete while others remain a mystery. Don't get discouraged—it's part of the process. Writing helps bring deep matters to the surface. It feels like therapy to me. You may even find you love it!

Take time to pause and reflect. Pay attention to what's stirring. Sit with the questions that arise. What unsettles you? Why? When a thought, question, or puzzle comes to mind, write it down. Allow it to be a springboard for more. Pursue wisdom and grace, and keep your heart open to learning. Use these moments to pause and pray, inviting God to guide you—even if you've never spoken to Him before.

Pray! If prayer is new to you, find a quiet, private place and explore this wonder. Prayer is simply acknowledging your spirit as part of your being and the God who created you. It's an act of humility and the doorway to a deeper life. It's done simply by talking to God—heart to heart. Invite Him to be part of your building process.

Prayer: God, I ask You to guide me through this journey and give me the words that will act like keys to open my heart to Your wisdom and love. Help me move into a new place of openness where I can imagine with greater clarity the hope You intend for my life. Amen (which means, let it be so).

Action Steps will be a continual component of this book, as wisdom only becomes wisdom when understanding is put into action. That's when we start to learn the ways of wisdom - when we practice it. Commit to the process and understand, you need to give yourself grace to grow. Grace for growth has been a personal tagline for me and has helped me press on when I felt like quitting. Give yourself grace to feel uncomfortable, discouraged, and puzzled, and yet still move forward to learn, change, practice, and become the best rendition of you. Build and keep building you!

Out of the Ashes

Have you ever stood on two sides of the same canyon? It's not a common thing. It takes tremendous effort to travel the distance to gain that perspective. As I write this book, that's how I feel. Twenty years ago, I stood on one side of life and thought it was over. I looked out over my angry soul, my broken heart, and the marriage, family, and faith I called my own. It was a mess, and I thought that's the way it would be—forever.

Twenty years later, I am amazed at the love, mercy, peace, and wisdom within me, my husband, and my children. We are not at the summit, but we are on the path, encouraging each other in life. How did this happen? That's what I'm about to share with you. This is the story of how, instead of trashing it all—my marriage, my family, and my faith—when I hit rock bottom, I looked up, prayed, and found the wisdom that would change my life—all our lives. All it required was a willingness to listen and follow the way of wisdom.

If you're holding this book, you might be searching for something—answers, direction, hope. I know that search well.

Years ago, I was standing in the rubble of my life: my heart was broken, my marriage was fragile, my household was stressful, and my future was uncertain. Then, in a single moment of prayer, I heard four words that would become my lifeline. They carried me through the darkest nights and gave me the courage to rebuild, piece by piece, brick by brick. These words are not just ideas; they are proven tools for transformation. They rebuilt my life, and I believe they can help rebuild yours.

This book is not just my story; it is a testament to the reality of God and the transforming power of wisdom. Even if you don't believe in God, read every chapter and challenge yourself to use the action steps as a guide. Draw from it. Wisdom works. Light drives out darkness. Dare to believe. Now for those four wonderful words.

An enormous hand-painted mural stands as the focal point in our bedroom. Like my life, I designed, built, and crafted that piece of art with my husband, Kevin—my dearest friend since my teens and lover for life. As you read the book, you'll discover that my current description of him is a miracle. I wasn't always so positive and grateful for him. What changed? It's a miracle created by four words. Those four words are the focal point in my bedroom, on that mural. It stands as a symbol reminding us that every day we are building this thing we call life. Whitewashed shiplap and golden stenciled words make up the mural, serving as a constant reminder that our lives are pliable, changeable, and buildable.

Humble, Grateful, Noble, Faithful.

The enormity of the piece goes along with my personality. I didn't coin the phrase "Go big or go home," but I'm sure I'm related to the author. The piece hangs almost floor to ceiling between two windows. I wanted it big, reminding me of the power of words. Even more, it reminds me of the power of God. I discovered these four words in prayer during a desperate chapter in my life. They saved my broken heart, our marriage, and family.

You may wonder why I am going on about the art in my bedroom. Believe it or not, those words are the reason I'm writing this book. They were also the reason I dedicated my life to helping people find hope, overcome adversity, and build their lives. The year-long project of writing this book is for you. I believe wisdom will lift you to a strength you never imagined.

Wisdom originates with God. He is the life force and Redeemer of those who have lost their lives to ignorance or pride. Yes! There is a God; He loves us and created us to live connected to Him. When we live in that divine plan, we have what the Hebrew translation of the Bible calls zoe life, a God quality of life. John 3:16. God created humanity with a spiritual core. It's His design and desire that we would be alive at the core level, filled with divine love and led by divine wisdom.

This is no bait and switch. This book is about the mystical aspect of our being, our spirit, and how we thrive when that core is alive. God gave us the choice to follow Him and His wisdom or go our own way. The story of Adam and Eve and the origins of humanity is found in the book of Genesis. Humanity chose rebellion. Though God could have abandoned us to the consequences of our choice, He chose a different response. He built a bridge back to the original hope. Anyone who says yes to this path back to life can return to living in His presence. Jesus, the Son of God, came to make that path clear, removing sin and shame. He invites us to choose the path of life and return to the Father's love and wisdom. This is the light that brings life back to our being.

My life was a mess hidden behind a facade. My marriage and family hung together by a thread. I was striving to make faith work in a soul stuck in a ditch dug out by lies, fear, and addiction (coping mechanisms for comfort). I believed in God, but had only seen His nature filtered and skewed through the lens of religion. My marriage weathered a tough period, one that persisted for more than ten years. I put my children first, but they grew up with a frazzled, scared, angry version of me. I was perpetually stumbling, year after year, longing for purpose and peace.

It took 42 years of life before I finally brought an end to the chaos and addressed my broken heart issues - alone with God. Everything was imploding. My heart was dragging around an emotional U-Haul of debris collected from tragedies throughout life. Those unattended traumas crushed my definitions of God, myself, and others. My life was in ruins.

Hiding in the rubble behind a veil constructed with the threads of a fierce work ethic, talent, and charisma, I banked my life on the facade. I trusted it to ensure love and approval. It worked. Spinning plates works! Others valued me, but for the wrong reasons. Those I served - loved me. They accepted me as long as I was jumping through their hoops. As long as the plates were spinning, I earned approval. The game eventually exhausted me, and the reality of my starving soul pushed me to an all-time low.

Disillusioned with religion, yet so convinced of God's existence, I quit church. Let me be clear: I abandoned everything that contributed to my false sense of self-worth and took a year-long break to pursue serenity. Some call it a sabbatical. That decision changed my life. I spent the entire year focusing on God's love, revealed in the Bible. Two things drove the sabbatical: accepting and addressing the reality of my broken heart and answering a divine call to find peace in God. The invitation was simple: pursue God alone for healing and hope and develop a new plan for life.

My life up to that point had been an enormous game of distractions, dodging unanswerable questions and ignoring a broken heart. Even the church was a distraction to me. It did nothing but antagonize and taunt me with the ongoing to-do list to be accepted. The grace we sang about didn't feel real. I felt the human version of it - conditional love. Deep within, I knew God's love and the grace I needed were far deeper and more powerful.

The shift from performance to grace seemed impossible. The only life I knew was based on score charts. This had to change if I was going to understand the Gospel and God's intent for living. A complete paradigm pivot was the only thing that would liberate me from performing for love to living from love. I'm going to say it again. I needed to see and understand God's love and wisdom accurately, so that I would quit performing for love and live from love.

Finally, one summer day, as I sat outside, reading Galatians chapter one, I felt a divine invitation to choose a different path, a different way to live. I sensed God's invitation. "Come away with Me." If you're not a spiritual person, that statement is going to seem crazy. But if life is crushing you, that invitation may sound like a ticket to hope. It was for me - and it is for you! It's a universal invitation God has been sending out throughout history. However it hits you, stick with me.

The beckoning voice called me to abandon my ladder-climbing tactics and make God's love my sole pursuit in life. The whole thing was very puzzling, and I questioned what I heard. For months, I did nothing in response but ponder it. Finally, the following January, I made a bold choice to quit all the programs I volunteered for and my quests for significance, everything. I decided it would be a year fully committed to knowing more about God.

For the month of January, I immersed myself in the Bible, researching and meditating on every verse that spoke of God's love for humanity. I made that study my number one quest, just like He invites us to in 1 Corinthians 14:1. It felt like my heart had entered a stream of mystical power. It had an amazing effect on me, erasing sorrows, stirring hope. What had occupied my intellect, knowing God was real and loved me, became something very different - a deep-planted conviction and belief.

Meditating on God's love, letting it fill and wash over our souls repeatedly throughout the day, gives truth time to move from the mind to the spirit. Information and inspiration are very different experiences. Piece by piece, God's love reconstructed and healed decades of what felt like ruins. The concept of being loved so completely built someone entirely new. Love lifted the rubble and sorrow until finally I could breathe.

This revelation of God's love awakened me. A famous line from an ancient story became my experience: All I know is that once I was blind, but now I can see. John 9:25 It's true! I gained an understanding that I hadn't had before. God's love inspired Him to create and redeem all things. He is love. The love emanating from God's heart resides within every element on earth. Every aspect of the universe and humanity itself is a creative expression of His love.

Love inspired God to create all that exists. And when humanity rebelled, in love, He pursued and redeemed us. God continually gives humanity the opportunity to find His goodness and live in His love. He will never cease to provide an on-ramp for those who walk in darkness.

As I followed His invitation and pursued knowing His love, I discovered the genuine person and nature of God. I also discovered myself. This two-sided discovery became the foundation of my life. It was the event that raised me out of the ashes. All the self-sabotage, sorrows, and losses that had burned my soul to the ground were suddenly overshadowed by a truth that became the defining factor of my life: God is real and He loves me. As I grew in the understanding of His love, I recognized a deep need for wisdom. It was in the pursuit, in the prayers for wisdom, that God gave me four magic words. They became pillars springing up from the foundation of love and wisdom—the four pillars that would rebuild my life: humble, grateful, noble, and faithful.

Action Steps

1. Set aside intentional time each day to seek God's love

Using Scripture and prayer, focus on your relationship with Him. Meditate on Bible verses about God's love for humanity until they move from head knowledge to heart conviction.

2. Identify and Name the Four Pillars in Your Own Life

Reflect on the four words — *Humble, Grateful, Noble, Faithful* — and begin practicing them daily. Journal about where each virtue shows up (or is missing) in your thoughts, relationships, and decisions. Ask God to teach you how to build with wisdom, reshaping your character and reclaiming peace and purpose.

3. Step Away to Heal

Create space — even if just an hour a week — to step back from performance-based living, religious routines, or toxic environments. Use that time to be honest with God about the condition of your heart. Make these moments happen, to be still, assess, and allow God to speak healing into your pain.

What's the Magic Word

Choosing the title of this book was a bit of a wrestle. I almost called it, What's the Magic Word? That title represented two realities that the book unfolds. First, our obsession with quick fixes, the fast track, and the microwave answers to life. We are trained to believe a pill is the answer to things that should be solved with a healthy lifestyle and that riches are found in the right numbers on a ticket. This paradigm is paralyzing to our culture and our potential. We want magical escapes from our conflicts, and they just don't exist.

There is, however, something magical, mystical, that does exist and works wonders in the lives of every person who finds and lives by it. The book unpacks the wonder of this kind of magic - what happens when we pivot from a fantasy land mindset to the true wonder of spirit-led transformation. The chapters ahead talk about the very real magic of listening to God. The wisdom of God has been recorded in the Bible and drawn from by great kings and leaders throughout history. This wonder is the magic, the power that, when applied to our lives, will turn our ashes into a thing of beauty.

There is profound wonder in the wisdom of God. He shares His wisdom wrapped in words. His words work wonders within the human soul. They transform our lives. It feels very magical to this day when I look back at the wonder unfolding in slow motion.

I know the word magic will offend some people. But there is reverence and wonder behind my use of it. When we think of magic, we often think of a fairy tale scene in the movies and a Bibbity, Boppity, Boo song that makes all the rags fall away and nothing but glory and glamour remains. But in real life, the wonder of transformation takes a little longer than one song. Wonder happens in a series of yes moments when we agree with God. It's a journey, a quest that takes us from rags to righteousness.

What does your dream look like? How would you describe the pinnacle of life? Strength, fulfilled dreams, healthy relationships, no regrets, peace, influence, wealth? There are a dozen different answers to those questions because we have different ideals, but the basics are the same. We often think the highest achievements involve conquering what we don't have and becoming the best versions of ourselves.

As I considered my life, I felt very much the same. I wanted to reach the summit of life and quit choking on the ashes of my last disappointment. In His goodness, God met me in those ashes and invited me up the mountain. That's what He's doing in your life, too. Do you hear that whisper of hope? Is your life quiet enough to hear His voice?

When I responded to that call and quieted my life, the discovery of strength through prayer and meditation was like a treasure map for life, and I couldn't get to the "X" fast enough. I just want to find the mother lode of peace and fulfillment, whatever it looks like. So, I continued in the pursuit of discovering more about God and myself through prayer, meditation, and exploring scripture.

Months passed, and I remained focused on His love. It became clear I needed more wisdom. God created the world with wisdom, and He provides that building block to anyone who asks for it. I asked. Prayer was an anchor point, like never before. In that season of surrender, I sensed words that felt like whispers in my heart - words of wisdom to help me find God - and peace. I saw wisdom in smaller blocks that would help me rebuild my life. These blocks were four words that I affectionately refer to as the magic words that brought me from the ashes into a beautiful place of peace. A Cinderella story.

God's version of a redemptive story is very different than the fairy tales we contrive. When God found me at the height of my private mess, I had been fantasizing for years about finding another guy and starting life over. I was unfaithful in my heart for years. My husband was a nice guy, but he was not present or emotionally intelligent. I wanted someone who was all that. Truth be told, I wasn't either. That gives you a fairly clear picture. Faithfulness was the summit of a mountain I could barely imagine.

Faithfulness was not my character. The top three virtues — Humble, Grateful, and Noble — were going to be my road to the ultimate goal of faithfulness.

To be honest, I thought it might take a month or two to nail it down. I'm a go-getter. Get it done! But that's not how it happened. It took several years before those virtues became defining elements of my character. Several years.

Faithful. The weight of the word is beyond my comprehension, greater than my imagination. The word defines the ultimate strength, not just for my marriage and family, but for my character and purpose. It was an aspiration that often left me feeling incapable and hopeless. I was used to faking it. Faithfulness is far from plastic. In those early years, I was deeply unsettled as a woman, wife, and mother, constantly carrying a sense of failure. Faithfulness seemed unattainable.

Feelings of insecurity and failure haunted my soul. Up to that point, nothing I had achieved had offered a deep sense of fulfillment. Nothing mattered. I was drowning in a sea of hopelessness. Though I experienced moments many would consider exciting, they offered only vapors of fulfillment, flickers of fame. They were only plastic idols, proving my ability to produce meaningless things. Success by the world's terms is empty and unsustainable. The applause vanished quickly, like a puff of smoke. These experiences only reinforced my discouragement and disappointment with myself, others, and life. They rubbed against the wound created by never feeling truly loved and cherished.

Faithful? It appeared to be an impossible dream. Up to that

point, it was merely a definition related to a hard work ethic. The virtue was empty because I was empty. I tried to gain the title of faithful the same way religion encourages: work harder at doing good, show up at church every Sunday, and give more money. Do, give, repeat, forever. Then you're deemed faithful. It's not only exhausting- it's not sustainable. Here's the big why: faithfulness is not a title referring to performance. Genuine faithfulness is a matter of deep character - it flows from the depths of love. It's love with loyalty.

Who else needs to hear this? Faithfulness is not a badge of honor for doing. It's a fruit of healthy living. When done for love, to earn approval, it's empty. In its beautiful, pure state, faithfulness flows from love. Some will only love you if. In that culture, those who hold the ruler or stand by the scales measure faithfulness by their demands. This doesn't represent God.

We were created and intended to live from love, not FOR love.

From love. A minute variation of words creates a world of difference. Love creates faithfulness.

When we work for love, we act like prostitutes, hustling for what's needed. That illustration fits into the file my husband and I call "True, but not nice."

It's a sad reality to think of any dear woman having to sell herself to survive. Even as I write it, there is a sting of sorrow within me. There are religious cultures based on performance, where love and connection are based on a fulfilled attendance and donation score. This should not be!

Jesus chewed out the Pharisees for this performance-based behavior. He told them to change their priorities to justice, mercy, and the love of God. Matthew 23:23. He warned his disciples about this tendency and said repeatedly, "Don't let that attitude get into you." Don't be like them. The culture of God's Kingdom is all about love and the goodness that flows from it. Connection and generosity will always flow through a person who lives from the perfect love of God - without measure. No human scorecard required.

We possess an inner knowing. That internal homing device craves the truth: We were created to receive and live from the love of God, to live from the power of love, and love Him in return.

God created us in His image to be loving, kind, noble, and faithful. Something in us knows we are noble by birth. The question is, will we go to God for this life-giving force of love and loyalty? Will we agree with His wisdom and ways? Or will we hustle for a lesser version of it so we can go our own ways and merely feed our ego? Resilient, unwavering faithfulness only results from a sustained life sourced from spiritual love and wisdom.

Truth be told, if we could make ourselves faithful, the work of Christ was unnecessary. Deep within, I recognized that true faithfulness went far beyond the superficiality of duty or empty loyalty. I knew there was more. But what? And how could I discover the truth? What would it take to move from a hustle-driven lifestyle to one centered on loving kindness that could not be shaken?

How do we establish a life of peace? How do we sustain that peace and live faithfully? It requires us to break free from the mindset made by impulsive choices and shallow living. A life of peace requires us to shift from our preferences to wisdom above our own. This is the core message I'm writing to you. And it isn't just my story; it's everyone's story. As I share mine,

I hope to bring light to your journey and the chapter you are wrestling to write today.

There are thousands of books pointing to God and offering hope. May this one add courage to your adventure. It's a journey - sometimes a battle. Whether you believe in God or are just exploring faith, you will find something in these pages that you can use for your quest.

We are all continuing to venture onto this mountain called life. Whether you are merely searching for spiritual clarity or have been navigating this road for decades and have the summit in sight, be open to growth. While you read, be self-aware. As your mind processes words, your heart is gathering ideas. Write them down!

The longer we focus on wisdom, the clearer things become. Wisdom has a way of stirring courage and lighting up the next step. Make it a daily practice to apply yourself to meditations of hope. It's like working out at the gym. Strength is gained incrementally. God will give you more and more understanding of His love and reveal the power of His promises. He will calm your fears as you focus on the truth.

He will win your heart and convince you that you are loved and He is faithful. As you spend time in prayer and meditation, you will sense Him working! Make this a life practice, and deep inner peace will become your culture.

To ensure I don't leave you wondering what happened to my marriage and kids, I'll share a current-day summary. My husband and I took the wisdom and grace found in these magic words and made them our guidelines for living and loving. We looked to God for grace to grow, to love each other fully in the present, but also to work for a better future. The once-broken, neglected state of our home has been on a growth journey ever since. We continue to work to make it a place filled with love, kindness, and joy. We work on ourselves as individuals and bring what we gather privately into our lives, marriage, and family. It's been a long journey, building love.

We have not arrived. The cultures we grew up in as children profoundly affected our ability to sense the needs of others and provide care as spouses, parents, and friends. Although we had wonderful parents, the culture has radically shifted over the past few decades. We have read, researched, and listened, gaining a far greater understanding of human needs, the impact of trauma, and the wisdom of emotional regulation and care. We had some catching up to do. We continue to work on the emotional intelligence skills required for great relationships. Neither of us is perfect. Neither of us has reached the fullness of wisdom, compassion, and maturity we aspire to, but we continue to follow the path of growth, love, and faithfulness.

Another important note. We returned to attending church. Here's what I took away from that long season of following Christ alone. Christians are meant to be people filled with the love and nature of God. Some people can do that in distracting settings, surrounded by a dozen voices. Some need a quieter setting to calibrate to God. We needed the quiet to get our souls rooted in our faith. Today, we are happy and ready to bring encouragement to others every time we walk in the door. We love to worship God with other believers and celebrate the goodness and wisdom of His Word.

A Common Battle

Despite all the progress that has been made over the years, a familiar foe occasionally resurfaces: Regret. The hardest part of becoming new is facing the temptation to look back and get stuck in remorse. We can't look back and move ahead. The rearview mirror temptation of regret is very real. The more we love our family, the harder it is to consider our failures. Shame tells us we will never be forgiven. That dark demon wants to chain us to the sorrow of regret. But the mercy of Christ forgives us of all sin and invites us to agree with God. We have to agree with Him to receive and live by His redeeming grace and move forward. There is a word in the Bible that is helpful to consider: Justified. This is what Christ accomplished for us on the cross. His redeeming work completely pardoned us of sin. This is huge! When I was a child, I learned the definition of the word with the statement, "Just as if I never sinned."

Regret is a giant that shows up occasionally on the battlefield of my soul. Can you relate? The vast majority of people battle it, whether it concerns something done or something we wish we had done. Regret can steal our attention and strength. If left alone, it hijacks real estate in our soul and attempts to build a monument of fear, a shrine of shame.

The years of brokenness in our hearts and marriage took a toll on our kids - just like my mother's brokenness affected me, and my husband's family issues affected him. Thankfully, we have three amazing people as our kids, and they are learning the same lessons of humility, gratitude, nobility, and faithfulness that their father and I work to gain. We have endured some very painful heart-to-heart conversations about the past, fighting to bring in mercy and choose forgiveness. I see my children making the same brave choices and rising with grace. Their choice to love and forgive me has been the greatest reward in life. Professor Emeritus, psychologist, author, and speaker, Dr. Jordan Peterson, sums up navigating regret so well. "If we don't deal with them properly, we will beat ourselves to death... Everyone makes mistakes... they need to treat themselves with mercy along with justice."

I do not doubt that God will continue to empower all of us, providing the wisdom and grace needed to navigate the challenges of marriage, family, and life. Together, we committed as a family to this journey. Just as Paul wrote, I am certain the One "who began the good work" within us will guide us and bring it to completion, making us people of great courage and grace - faithful. Philippians 1:6. May our story of restoration, along with the inspirational writing, fuel your courage and bring you great hope for the future. I hope it will help you rise stronger, commit to the quest, and live with love and loyalty - faithful.

Action Steps

1. Trade Performance for Presence

In your daily practice of morning calibration, focus on this: I spend this time not to "earn" anything from God, but to *be* with Him. This cultivates your awareness of the life He intended: *presence over performance.*

2. Replace Regret with Mercy

Identify one area where regret weighs on you. Write a declaration of mercy over that memory. Write down one step you can take to move forward today.

Regret paralyzes, but mercy liberates and helps us move forward. Choosing mercy isn't denial — it's agreeing with God's truth over shame. He prefers mercy over judgment. Practice this in your own heart. It will prepare you to bring mercy to others.

The Wonder of Words

At this very moment, you are living by invisible words. Though invisible, they are powerful. These words act as magicians. Applied with diligence, your words become your reality. Those words are the prophets of your next step, trainers determining the strength you will live by. Those invisible words are the ones you choose by default or deliberately. They are the builders of your attitude and designers of your future. Do you know what your invisible words are? If not, take the pulse of your feelings and survey your habits. They are the amplifiers of thought.

Thoughts are tools, and great thoughts build a great life. If you commit to the process I'm about to share, you will look back in total amazement at what your life has become. I am bringing 20 years of life coaching to print to help people build their lives. My goal is to encourage you to see and start building a vibrant life with the simple tools that make the biggest difference.

Becoming is a process, and wisdom is the way we get there.

Wisdom is the highest form of thinking. You may wonder what the connection is between wisdom and the book's title. I use the term "Magic Words" because transforming our lives creates a sense of wonder. The pliability of our lives is astonishing—and possible! I will unveil some of these magic marvels as we go through the chapters.

You are already carrying unspoken words that are forming beliefs, holding the magic, and prophesying your future. What are some of those words? What are the hidden messages that have been defining who you are and what you do? These are your beliefs about yourself, life, others, and God. What are they? Quiet yourself for a moment. Consider what thoughts recur and pull you down. Consider the thoughts you have had that lift you. We will return to this later.

Our First Magic Word

As little children, we learned the power of one simple word. When activated, we became witnesses to its wonders. One word could change our circumstances, open doors, and provide what we need. It was amazing to experience the impact of that one magic word. Occasionally, when I forgot to use the magic word when requesting an item or help with a project, my parents and teachers would hold me to it with this gentle prodding: What's the magic word? The answer, of course, was "Please".

We all know firsthand the power of the word - please. Those who remember to use the word "please", exhibiting grace and humility, are the ones we are most happy to help. Doors open for people who say please. Kindness seems to flow toward those who carry a humble attitude and speak the word. That magic word expresses an attitude of graciousness, a characteristic that never loses its appeal. It applies to both children and adults. How can one word possess so much power? The truth is, all words possess power. All words are meaningful, but please is exceptional as it expresses an attitude of humility.

Words are powerful, like mini GPS systems, and tiny engines driving and guiding conversations and attitudes. Words are like plows that make the soil ready for the next step or season in life. Words can produce light and hope. They can also shut down a soul and bring belief to a crushing end. There is so much power within words. For better or worse, our soul follows the stream of that power. The soul follows spoken words, either up or down. Our cultural climate of negativity, sarcasm, fear, and doubt fills the airways and our minds, even coming out of our mouths. The result is this: our soul follows the message we feed on and turns our speech up or down. It guides our perspectives, expectations, and decisions with the same force.

Words pour in and shape us. The themes we gather set our inner compass. That compass creates behavior. Left unchecked, behavior becomes a habit. Unless something interrupts the cycle, the common sound of cynicism taints our entire lives. We live with less hope, less energy for the tasks in life, and tire easily, mentally and physically. Without hope, we give up what matters most in our relationships and work.

It all begins with the words we allow to shape our world. Words possess that much power. We can feel them at work, affecting our lives, adding or removing strength. We can take control of the whole downward spiral and flip it! We can turn it upward by changing our thoughts and reforming our words.

Not only do the words we hear and say energize us, but they shape us by impressing ideas and perspectives into our souls.

The words we listen to have the power to craft our character and sculpt our senses.

Aligning our conversation by filtering our words and choosing positivity strengthens us. Fear or faith, greed or kindness, evil or good, darkness or light - words carry the virtues that determine our values and prophesy our potential. They can harm or heal us.

This book aims to inspire and encourage you to develop spiritual wellness by tending to the words you allow in your ears, heart, and mouth. I hope to encourage you to become more vigilant than ever about pursuing wisdom and being inspired by love. Love and wisdom are the most potent virtues in life: restoring, forging, and feeding our strength. Further virtues inspired by love and wisdom have the power to build every aspect of our lives.

Most of us function with an outside-in paradigm, living in response to circumstances rather than guided by our inner compass. We live more aware of problems than of our potential, moved by the grind of life, rather than by the grace within. It's common to think from merely a physical, visible, and tangible level. We think personal resources solve problems. We may believe in resources and may think and say: If I only had more money. I think we've all said that at one point. But the actual key to building a great life is not what's in our hands, but what's in our hearts.

When we live from a deeper place, we discover more about our potential. Reactionary living is the status quo. Physical matters are much easier to survey and understand, so we make them the top priority. This makes us trigger-happy, settling for a reactionary lifestyle. It's debilitating because clarity and conviction require insight and honesty. A healthy belief system is more important than a billion dollars. Money will not solve problems.

What will bring our lives to a state of true peace? God holds the answer. Each one of us is unique in his or her hunger and frustrations, thirst and needs. God knows each one and how to satisfy our lives completely. Time spent in silent reflection, prayer, and meditation, focusing on and pondering wisdom, love, and peace, will transform us. This time of quiet each day allows our souls to calibrate to God's wisdom and grace. He knows exactly what we need and has hidden it within the Bible. Quiet meditation on the scriptures speaks volumes and inspires worship. God knows how to address the emptiness, the questions, and the chaos, and lead us into peace. This type of living requires us to turn off the screens and quit replaying the reels of anger or complaints looping in our minds concerning work or home, where the fires are blazing. It requires us to quiet our setting and center our souls.

Can you feel it? Can you sense the thing inside that tells you to live beyond circumstance? The peace you long for is a divinely placed hunger drawing you to Him. He is leading you into peace to fill you with hope. It's God's design for you to be light and carry hope; a deep well of wisdom and love - for your enjoyment and to bring light into your world. It's a powerful centering thing and what we long for - peace. To know and love God and to bring His light to the world fulfills two deeply ingrained needs of understanding and purpose. When we commit to these two primary callings, we discover ourselves and find fulfillment.

God is love, and He is light. The whole point of Christ's coming to Earth was to redeem us and lead us into the light, where we know the Father and discover our true nature: love and light. If this story is new to you, stop at this point and read the book of John in the Bible. Read it a few times this week to allow it to become clearer. John does a great job unpacking the Gospel.

An innate core conviction exists within us, looking for something bigger than ourselves. This hunger is a whisper of our spirit. This is God's homing device, pointing us to Him. Mathematician and physicist, Blaise Pascal, describes it this way: "A God-shaped vacuum exists in the heart of every man, which no created thing can fill, but only God the Creator, made known through Jesus Christ." Acknowledging this core-level hunger opens us to the Gospel and the gift of the Holy Spirit.

The Bible further explains the wisdom of this core need. It describes God as the Rock of Ages, a name well-suited. Whoever lives by His wisdom and love becomes unshakeable. The nature of the Rock of Ages becomes our nature. Each of us will face storms: depression, hardship, loneliness, loss, disillusionment, betrayal, lack, and fear. These are part of the common human experience. Yet, in each of those dark valleys, we can rise above the circumstances. We can build an unshakeable life.

This standard of living from the inside out is the highest form of strength. God fills our spirit and soul, which energizes the body. We need to look only to our physical self to understand how this core strength functions. Many people work on their health and physique, developing strength and agility in their arms and legs. One of the most commonly ignored aspects of training concerns the core. It's true mentally and emotionally as well. People live unaware of their spirit, neglecting their core.

In athletics, trainers and therapists refer to the core region as the posterior and anterior chains. The posterior chain is the segment of the body comprising muscles on the backside of the body, including the glutes, hamstrings, calves, erector spine, lats, and rear delts/shoulder muscles. This is an enormous amount of our body's mass, making up half of our musculature. It is the source of our core strength. Working in cooperation with the anterior chain enables us to walk upright, bend, move, and function in daily life. If maintained through exercise and an active lifestyle, our posterior and anterior chains will keep us limber and capable throughout life. Neglected and ignored, a weak core results in back and hip issues, which translates to pain. Our body mechanics illustrate how the spirit works. Neglected, we are weak. Developed, we are strong and flourish in life. Pain is often a sign of an undeveloped core.

The spirit is to our being what the posterior chain is to our body. We are unaware of its existence until we experience the pain of neglect. As we develop our posterior chain through weight training, strength increases. The improved muscle structure often results in the reduction or elimination of pain. Activating our spiritual core leads to this outcome of strength. This is not about going to church. Many people attend a church with minimal transformation in their souls. Transformation is the result of a daily choice, not a weekly tradition.

The Bible encourages developing this core level of our being and points us to the truth: God provides strength. It reads: Deep calls out to deep. Psalm 42:7 Our spiritual need for God is a profoundly divine matter. That hunger is a divinely planted setup, drawing us to respond to Him. My favorite reminder of this comes from Ecclesiastes 3:11, which reads, "He has made everything beautiful in its time. He also has planted eternity in men's hearts and minds [a divinely implanted sense of a purpose working through the ages which nothing under the sun but God alone can satisfy]..." from the Amplified version of the Bible. This reminds us that there is something vast and profound within us, and no trivial thing on earth is going to fill that hunger, but God alone.

Our hunger for life is an echo of God's message, reflecting His desire to create a divine version of life within us. We must not neglect this. We cannot neglect this and expect to live a life of peace. The hunger demands a response. We must meet the cry of our soul with openness to His wisdom, looking to His Word for the path of life.

The simple practices of prayer, meditation on the wisdom of the Bible, and practicing humility in daily choices guided by love and grace, as we agree with God, cultivate the strengthening of our souls. We become strong and unshakeable through daily disciplines and continual moments of agreement with grace. As we commit to training, our souls will become clear, strong, and resilient. This is the path to developing deep core strength.

You can do this. I can do this. The Holy Spirit is our trainer and source of strength. These spiritual, private practices lift our hearts to think, believe, reason, and function like our Father, God. When our souls flourish, every aspect of our lives is affected. Paul said it this way: "I pray you would prosper and be in health, even as your soul prospers." 3 John 1:2

As I write this, I am aware of the broad spectrum of beliefs within the readers. Some of you, having faced years of battles and victories, may hold a strong spiritual conviction and know these things well. While some readers ponder the meaning behind this spirit-core matter, and are searching for what they believe. That's okay! It's awesome that you're willing to explore. Keep searching.

For years, I've lived by a simple phrase: Don't settle for the title of expert; be an explorer. No matter where you are on the spiritual spectrum, as you pick up this book, open your heart to the possibilities God wants to gift to you. He designed us to be creative, innovative, and adventurous. He redeemed us into an amazing, continually expanding experience of life. Let your uncertainty and tendency to wrestle help you find more of God.

I have served as a coach to hundreds of people over the past two decades. I often encourage people in their development, with this thought: Spiritual growth is invisible and mysterious. Because we don't fully understand it, we feel clumsy, sometimes uncomfortable. Because of the discomfort, you may be tempted to ignore spiritual matters. Don't ignore it. Your spirit is the core of your being. You wouldn't stop eating because you didn't understand nutrition. You eat because, without food, you will die. Your spirit is a part of your being, and when cared for, it brings life.

Confront the clumsy questions. Wrestle toward God, not away from Him! God honors every step we make, exploring who He is and the wonder of His Word. You will feel your spirit come to life, and your experience of life will expand as you continue to explore the spiritual reality of your life in the light of God's love.

Action Steps

1. Identify Your Invisible Words

Spend 10–15 minutes in quiet reflection. Write down the beliefs and phrases you often hear internally. Which ones give you strength? Which ones weaken your spirit?

2. Align Your Words With God's Wisdom

Do your words reflect fear or faith, reaction or revelation? What words of hope have you found in scripture? Rewrite the script you are acting from throughout the day. Agree with God.

This isn't about feelings. This is about setting the compass and changing direction. Feelings will follow later.

Choose one core area (marriage, parenting, work, or health) and intentionally speak words of blessing into it for 7 days. Use a sticky note, journal, or voice memo to track changes in how you speak and how you feel.

3. Cultivate Core Strength Through Daily Stillness

Is your life too loud to hear the truth of who you are? This chapter reveals how your spiritual core—like the physical posterior chain—must be developed for resilience and movement. Your inner life needs intentional training and nourishment. God's voice, His "magic words," restore and reinforce identity, peace, and clarity.

Set aside a daily 10-minute quiet time for soul calibration.

Exploring the Magic

Thank you for sharing these chapters of my life and, in a way, sharing your life as you're willing to read the book and explore spiritual growth through this labor of love. We may not agree on everything - that's okay. Here's what I bring: Inspiration to explore. Be willing to think outside your box. Be open to more! Life provides a passageway for all of us to become bigger-hearted and open-minded. I hope this book helps you on that journey.

Second, let this book bring encouragement. No matter where you are, what chaos you call life, no matter how impossible the notion of peace appears, it's not. Twenty years ago, I was miserable, angry, alone, and ready to leave my husband - I just didn't know how. I didn't want to destroy our lives. I didn't want my kids to be crushed by the devastation of a divorce. I was afraid of losing our friends. I was miserable and ignorant of how to change the circumstances.

Thankfully, my desperation led me to listen to God and open my life to His wisdom. Little did I know that four simple words would reform my entire soul and every detail of my life. They became the pillars that God used to lift me out of the ashes of multiple losses and out of the cloud of confusion concerning my value and purpose in life. I was about to experience the pivot of a lifetime.

Here's a bonus to all this goodness. Hope is just as contagious as the sticky cynicism out there. Even more! Our soul longs for hope, and when we see it working, simply and authentically, in the lives of others, it appears possible for us, too. That's exactly what happened to us. Those magic words didn't stop with me. My husband witnessed the hope and wisdom that reformed my personality and approach to living. God was drawing him to hope and to change, too. God inspired him to rethink his mindset and grow as well. And the hope cycle continues as we share our story with others. Hope is transferable.

Slowly, we took on the pages of our marriage where we were neglectful because of fear, past wounds, or ignorance. Today, we are living in a real-life love story that we write together. We have a fun, loving, generosity-based marriage - beyond my dreams. We are still very human and tread cautiously into conversations where we were once weak, but we take them on and fight for each other, not against each other.

I welcome you to read and share my journey, and while you do, brave your story, flip through the pages of your life, spend time in prayer, and explore the wonder of what could be in your life. Imagine the possibilities these magic words hold for you. Though it may not be your current convictions, beliefs, or behavior, I hope you will draw gold from the shared treasures and benefit from the principles shared. Dare to be open-hearted and ask God to fill that space within you.

Every one of us benefits from the virtues of love and wisdom. Love is undeniably the universe's most powerful force, representing the very essence of life. God is love. It's a little baffling to consider that there is an embodiment of love. There is a mystery to the magic. Go beyond your understanding. Allow yourself to venture into the exploration of these spiritual things.

God is the embodiment of wisdom. We can find information, inspiration, and transformation in the Bible. They are powerful steps available for us as we build our lives. This is what He wants for all of us. Are you willing to slow yourself down to listen and let God breathe into your life? His wisdom will resuscitate your soul and lift the lid on your life. It's nothing short of magical. Our souls become buoyant when filled with the breath of God.

God downloaded His thoughts, hope, wisdom, and peace to share them with us. These words have the power to work wonders wherever they are shared. Some will hate that I am calling them magic words, considering it irreverend. It's not - it's childlike. To consider that He hovered over darkness and spoke a word, and created light is miraculous, magnificent, and magical. Maybe it's time we redeem words that restore the wonder of His power and goodness.

His words lift the ceiling and create a haven for our lives. Perhaps best of all, His words are eternal in virtue, power, and potential. They won't just last for a month - they will bring hope and peace for a lifetime and into eternity. God's Word is "self-fulfilling." Isaiah 61:11 Amplified Version. The Words of God, recorded in the Bible, are embedded with goodness, giving them the power to do what He intended. When He says light, there's no chance for darkness. The Word becomes His vision. He will keep His Word and prove to every heart that explores this wonder. His wisdom is higher than all the wisdom on Earth. It is pure magic.

Making it Your Own

The magic words I sought in prayer and discovered as gifts from God became the pillars I needed to restore my life. God is continually offering wisdom to anyone who will listen. The book of Proverbs compares wisdom to a woman who stands out in the marketplace, offering wisdom for everyone to hear. She calls out for all to hear. This represents the truth: God never stops offering us wisdom. Think about that truth as you navigate life. Let the book inspire you, prompting prayer, encouraging the pursuit of wisdom, and stirring hope. It's crucial to make space for these spiritual experiences.

Write words of inspiration in the margins. Journal phrases that feel like energy to fuel hope. I included Bible verses for inspiration in each chapter - search them out. If you don't own a Bible, consider buying one. The Readers Edition, New Living, and NIV are standard versions. I often share the Amplified Bible, as it unpacks meanings with more description than other translations. It's just not an easy, smooth read. There are also great apps like The Bible App. I like to have something offline. It feels more intimate out in the woods or on a mountain trail (my favorite quiet place). My biggest hope is this: Make this book an experience, not another book on the shelf, but a moment in your life. And make the Bible your key to knowing and understanding God.

Though you could read the book in a day or a weekend, I would suggest considering a slower pace to allow reflection. After all, it's not my inspiration that will reform your life - it's the spiritual wisdom that you will gather through reflection and prayer. If you read it slowly and journal through the process, you will gain so much more!

Gather your magic words of encouragement and keep them visible in your bathroom or bedroom, where you can ponder and pray, as you are guided by them. Keep that action-set practice going for months - even years. Gather the inspiration that will help you develop your inner strength. Allow this to be more than a book, but a moment in your life when you made a pivot toward peace. The winds of change require us to course-correct often. We will make several pivots in life. Learning to set our souls on wisdom and the love of God will help us pivot continually toward peace.

Yes, Please!

Looking at the first magic word of our childhood, please, I remember the obligation it appeared to be. It wasn't until I was an adult that I realized the real magic behind that word. Please encapsulate an attitude. It reveals a heart's posture. It's an inner light, signaling the character of the person speaking the word. Think about a time when someone carried that grace. Recall their tone of voice and body language. Can you feel the air around that moment, energized with humility? Ah, yes, there it is. The real magic within the word please is humility.

The nuclear power within "please" is humility. It expresses meekness, a humble statement acknowledging that one of us is not as strong as all of us. A heartfelt plea for help, expressed in word and tone, can create a bond of unity. It's a beautiful thing to watch. It's a gentle request we make to each other, creating a moment to meet at the table of life. We share the joy of partnership and generosity, followed by another beautiful phrase: thank you. These magic words teach us, move us, and remind us that such magic moves the world. It changes circumstances. And the genuine wonder is not magic but humility.

These two words have deep significance when we allow them to guide our lives. They are virtues. Virtues define moral character and construct noble lives. They contain the power to lift the nature of those who prioritize and practice them. One definition of virtue describes it as a beneficial power; another says strength or courage. Considering these definitions, it's clear that virtues are the cellular-level fiber that creates hope and peace. They are something we all need. Virtues change our everyday experience in every aspect of life. Who among us would not value more strength - mentally, emotionally, physically, and spiritually? This invisible power can transform any life, like magic. But to benefit from its flow, we need to find the source.

The books that form the Bible are the oldest in human history. Throughout every generation, from the dawn of time, its wisdom has been the guiding force for the free world, shaping the minds of powerful and wise individuals. These are ancient truths rooted in scripture, inspired by God. Every virtue finds its origin in the wisdom of God.

In the book of Proverbs 31, we read: "A capable, intelligent, and virtuous woman is worth more than rubies." This chapter about women describes the heart, mind, attitude, and lifestyle of virtue. Virtue crafts the pillars of her character. They are the secret of her hidden power, enabling her to live and love well. That entire chapter is inspiring as it describes a great king and a noble woman. These verses were written thousands of years ago to guide the reader, King Solomon, and they apply well to us today. When we listen to and apply wisdom to our lives, we lead ourselves, our families, and our workplace into peace. It's not a question of if it will happen, but when. Give it time. Like a flame in the fireplace, virtue turns an ember into an inferno. Just keep breathing and watch it rise.

God is the source of all wisdom. Wisdom is a spiritual fire looking for a stove to carry it. It gives us insight into the specific directives required to lift our imploded life, or to raise the roof on a whole new level. Wisdom builds things.

Throughout the book, I will share the words I discovered through prayer and meditation - words that became the source of hope to change my life, marriage, family, and work. I will unpack the magic discovered in each virtue and how it affects our lives. These words will provide power and encouragement as you read them. How can I make this bold claim? Because they aren't my words. They are virtues - sources of power. They are the thoughts God shares with us to lift our lives. The

Bible says God watches over His Word to perform it. Jeremiah 1:12 It also says His Word will not return to Him until it completes its mission. Isaiah 55:11. He sent His Word and healed us. Psalm 107:20.

You may read this book, unsure if you want to buy into the Christian faith because of what you've seen of the people who claim to believe in it. That's okay. This is a journey, not an event. Stay open. God wants you to know that you are dearly loved. Even if you don't believe, today, He will continue to send His message of hope to you. You can count on it! For the rest of your life, the endless echo of Heaven will say: God is love. He is real. And He loves you. He will never cease to express His love because He knows it's our lifeline to hope. Love delivers all the hope we need. Hope is oxygen. He is breathing hope into every life - your life and mine.

Turn your attention away from distractions, including people, negative news, and hype, and focus on Jesus. He's the only one who can spark faith and hope within you. He will walk with you through the valleys and along the summits, making your faith resilient. Forget the past and forge ahead with hope in Jesus. His love and courage restore the soul.

All words begin as thoughts. Just like food, words hold a value, calories, and nutrients, if you will. The quality of our food affects our health and strength. The quality of our thoughts shapes our conversations and, more importantly, our beliefs. Our words reflect the thoughts simmering in our souls. Thoughts processed - turn into beliefs. Broken lives are always caused by broken beliefs. The good news is we can redeem broken places. The way we think forms the words used to create beliefs that will shape our lives. We can reform the broken places by replacing failing words with words of life.

David wrote these words thousands of years ago, compelling Solomon to reach for greatness as king. "As a man thinks in his heart, so is he." Proverbs 23:7 This fatherly wisdom holds the same power today. God continually calls us to this lifestyle, directing our minds to His. Isaiah 55:8-9 states: "My thoughts are higher than yours." In Jeremiah 33:3, we read: "Call on Me, and I will tell you great and unsearchable things that you don't know." This is an amazing promise! Almighty God invites us to ask for the hidden wisdom needed to build a noble life and understand the mysteries in ourselves and life. What a promise!

Ready to raise the lid on your life? Which pillars are best suited for the task? Pray and ask God for this hidden wisdom. Commit to it daily in prayer and in pursuing wisdom in reading, listening to wise people, and recording what you read and hear. We need God's lid-lifting thoughts.

When you feel overwhelmed, challenge the assumptions guiding your life. Have you been living compelled by fear, anger, jealousy, envy, greed, or pride - unwilling to listen to wise counsel? Have you been limiting your life to a kiddie-sized thought pool? We were intended to live in God's ocean of wisdom, but we settle for a small existence, swimming in the little pool of our emotional and spiritual intelligence. God invites us to the deep.

Quit guarding the leaks in your life. If it's not creating peace, it's not right. We believe it's all about circumstances, but it's not! There is no circumstance stronger than wisdom, diligence, and a resolute human soul, surrendered to the Spirit.

Here's how resolved is formed. It happens in private. Start each day with the spiritual disciplines of prayer and meditation on God's Word. Wash your soul in silent or songful worship, allowing the goodness of God to create the rock of resolve within you. When the day begins with core care, daily circumstances will feel and unfold differently. What happens in the secret place doesn't stay secret for long. Spiritual strength is not something we put on. It's something God puts in us when we commit to humbling ourselves in sacred trust in the secret place. He enlarges our souls and lifts the ceiling with His love and wisdom. Everything within us rages against this stillness and discipline. But only in surrender do we discover the power to rise stronger.

Remove the Obstacles

As you read, be self-aware. If you feel an obstacle in the way, don't ignore it. You may be angry with yourself or someone else. You may be angry with God. Address the obstacle. Bitterness works against us. Forgiveness works for us. Forgiveness takes the hurdles, walls, and even mountains down. Though it may feel off-topic, it's important to address the obstacles. Guilt, sorrow, and shame can stop progress, and they don't need to, so confront them.

Guilt in the form of conviction is a pain that tells us to quit acting selfishly. When you hear it, respond. Quit living selfishly. Selfishness promises strength but delivers nothing. It robs us of hope. Admit where you've been thinking, speaking, or acting out of selfishness. Ask God to forgive you. Tell yourself the truth: Selfishness is costing me more than I want to pay. What I want is freedom, love with loyalty, and a life of peace. Selfishness won't get me there. I repent.

Sorrow is a natural reaction to loss. It's an appropriate response to loss. It should only last for a window of time. When I was a child, my dad died. Our grief was intense for a period, but we learned to move on. We still miss him, but sorrow has given way to hope. Prolonged sorrow can be a broken-hearted issue. Be cautious of allowing sorrow to become a personality trait. The Eeyore attitude. A spirit of heaviness is not sorrow. A spirit of heaviness is depression created by lies adopted as truth. Beliefs like, this will never change. God helps other people but not me. When we make the loss a permanent station, we have stopped following hope and surrendered to fear.

Christ came to heal the brokenhearted by revealing the truth. He can give our broken hearts a profound pivot into genuine joy. If that sounds like what you need, dig into the Bible, find the promises of healing and hope, and post those verses around your living spaces. When we know the truth, we find freedom.

Shame is entirely different from sorrow, though it can feel a lot like it. Shame is a type of grieving. But shame results from carrying guilt that doesn't belong to you. The Bible tells us, There is no condemnation or shame for those who are in Christ Jesus. Romans 8:1 He has paid for all the sin, guilt, and shame of humanity forever. Shame is a lie. Once we release our guilt and commit our hearts to Christ, there is nothing to be ashamed of. This is the promise for those who follow Christ.

Shame tells us we deserve punishment, and until we get it, we should punish ourselves internally. Do not agree with this dark message! Agree with God. Shake off shame and allow grace to work its wonders in and around you. Human grace is limited. God's grace is amazing - and more than enough for every struggle in our lives.

Shame is not something to allow in your life, ever. You may have heard the statement, "Shame on you." It's a manipulative phrase used by those who seek to control others. They are trying to create conviction, but conviction doesn't come through shaming. That's not the way God works in our hearts.

Stay away from people who try to manipulate by using that phrase. They do not represent God. God's kindness creates a healthy, motivating conviction that inspires us to see the better way and pivot by the power of grace. God will tell you the truth to redeem you, with love to empower you. No shame required.

Conviction is not shame. Conviction is like cold water in the face or smelling salts. It creates a startle and stimulates the spirit to awaken us to the reality of danger. Conviction is not related to shame. Don't be afraid of conviction. We need it. God does not shame people into repentance. He draws them in with kindness. Romans 2:4. And within that kindness, He tells us the truth, providing a startling moment to awaken us to impending danger. He leads us to walk in the light where shame cannot exist. 1 John 1:7.

Remove the obstacles. When something feels like it won't budge: guilt, shame, sorrow, anxiety, depression — do your best and trust God with the rest. Stay diligent in the disciplines of prayer and meditation on God's Word. That's our part. Ask God to move what you can't budge. He will answer.

God will help you and lift you into new strength. He will comfort your sorrow. The Bible reminds us of His promise to restore what is lost, stolen, and broken. He is the Prince of Peace. Isaiah 9:6. Peace comes from the Hebrew word shalom, which refers to a state of being where nothing is missing or broken.

Bringing Down Obstacles with Prayer

Pray what feels like a genuine expression for you. Forgiveness is the starting point of removing what hinders openness. Begin by removing what is in your soul. Second, pray for what hinders peace in your relationships with people. Finally, address any grudges or obstacles you have held between you and God. Forgiveness is the vital first step. Think about this step, and you will find comfort. Forgiveness does not come from your feelings. Feelings follow the choice of forgiveness. Forgiveness is the conviction that our lives will only grow when we let it go. Release the weight of your shame and the decisions that caused it. Forgive people and release them to God. Trust Him for the restoration of all things.

Prayer:

Father, forgive me for every foolish action, attitude, and word. Father, I forgive others for the foolishness in their lives. I will release them to You. I trust You for the restoration I need to live at peace. I will not look to people any longer. Peace comes from You.

Father, forgive me for being angry with You. You didn't do what I expected, and I was angry. I admit I don't see the big picture. I know You can restore and make something beautiful out of these ashes. Help me overcome doubt, fear, bitterness, and unbelief. Amen.

Action Steps

1. Name the Block:
Take 10–15 minutes in silence and prayer to identify any emotional or spiritual obstacle currently hindering your peace (e.g., anger, guilt, shame, grief). Write it down clearly in your journal or notebook. Naming the obstacle is the first step to disarming its power.

2. Choose Forgiveness Daily:
Write a short, personal prayer or affirmation declaring your willingness to forgive others, yourself, or even release frustration toward God. Repeat it aloud or in your heart each morning this week as a declaration of freedom.

3. Post a Truth That Heals:

Find one Bible verse from the segment (such as *Romans 2:4* or *1 John 1:7*) that speaks to your current obstacle. Write or print it on a sticky note and place it where you'll see it. Let that truth wash away the lies, shame, or sorrow in your soul.

The Real Magic

Who doesn't wish they could have a Cinderella story moment in their lives? It's human nature to want in an instant what is built over decades. In the big-screen Cinderella story, magic is a fictional experience involving a fairy godmother and a magic wand. You would think we outgrow these stories, but it's very common for adults to put their hope in fictional fantasies. When people don't know the goodness of God, they use a lottery-ticket lifestyle to build their lives.

In the movie, the fairy tale scene presents useless words that promise change. All you need is to put meaningless things together and use the "Bibbity, Boppity, Boo" song. Tadah! Your ragged existence suddenly becomes one of glory and glamour. In real life, the wonder of transformation takes much longer than one catchy song. And the words that create the change are far from meaningless. Wonder emerges from the ashes as we agree with the wisdom of God. Exchanging our thinking for His thoughts is the secret to transformation. It's a journey, a quest that takes us from the ashes to awe.

Imagine what God has in mind for you: a healthy life, with relationships, plans, and purposes that are filled with wisdom, peace, and joy. Let it take shape in your mind. Begin to practise healthy imaginations. Imagine the strength, peace, inner healing, fulfilled dreams, healthy relationships, courage, purpose, and joy of a God-given dream.

Does it feel impossible? It's not. But there needs to be a reality bridge to your dreams. A dream is a building project, not a fairy tale. As we unpack the wisdom needed to help you build that bridge, let me inspire you with a healthy perspective on a dream. Dreams are divine purposes. They are assignments from God. Dreams are always about discovery, service, and redemption. That's how you know it's from God. Pursuing them calls us to a path revealing more of God, our potential, and the great experiences in life. It will stretch us and hear this: dreams serve others. Building your life well involves building those around you.

God helps us build this life of fulfilled dreams. Again, it's not a fairy tale. It's a building plan. It will feel impossible as He always calls us to things that are way over our heads. That ensures our connection to Him in the work. Relationship will always be the top priority with God. You may have heard it said before: if your dreams don't feel way beyond you, they're not big enough. Dreams are bigger than us and are given to enlarge our lives so that God can fit into them.

Let me also repeat this point: There's a big difference between fantasies and dreams. Dreams are enormous plans that will take a lot of wisdom and work. They have several components: a partnership with God, a commitment to gain wisdom, a devotion to service, and a surrender to the process. This is dreamland! Not the one people rave over, but the real one that builds amazing lives.

Fantasies are quite different. They bank on ridiculous lottery-type events, little to no work, warped ideas, overnight gambles, and a lack of character. People who fantasize don't ask for counsel. They already know it all. If you were indoctrinated with this mentality, don't worry. You can shake it off and start fresh.

Don't get lost in the "bippity, boppity, boo" mindset. Don't tell yourself "God told me it was okay..." if it's not in line with His character or will to begin with. He will give you dreams that bring you peace and invite others to join. It won't be an easy road, but it will be simple. Pray, listen, test the plan, and trust the Lord. And, get wise counsel before making big decisions. Proverbs 24:6. These are the trade secrets of scripture. They've worked for kings and warriors throughout history. They will work for you.

It's easy to get sucked into the cultural mindset of lottery cards and diet pills, and everything else that has a microwave outcome. As I considered my life, I felt very much the same. I wanted to reach the summit of life and quit choking on the ashes of my last disappointment. By the age of thirty, I wanted everything figured out, but that didn't happen. I wanted to find my fairy godmother and recite the magic words with her. But God interrupted that futile thinking to give me wisdom. In His goodness, He met me in those ashes and invited me up the mountain. That's what He's doing in your life, too.

Do you hear that whisper of hope? Is your life quiet enough to hear His voice? I'm going to say it again: Don't make this a quick read. Make this a moment in your life. You will spend at least eight hours today building someone else's business or organization, or checking off assignments for school.
Don't neglect investing in your life. Build You!

From Fantasy to Reality

The wisdom of God is a measureless span of profound wonder. The Bible tells us that the wisdom of God formed all of creation. Proverbs 3:19, Jeremiah 51:15, and Proverbs 8:22-31. If that wasn't baffling enough, consider this: He shares His wisdom with humanity and wraps it in words. This same formative power of God's Word can be the guiding force of our lives. The creative power of God redeems us, working wonders within the human soul. It feels very magical to this day when I consider the mess I had made of my life before His Word made everything new.

When I decided to bring my life to an abrupt stop and go to work on myself, everything changed. It was a hard pivot. The abruptness provided extra gumption to face change. No one likes change. We tell ourselves we do, but let's be real. Change that builds a successful, healthy life is hard, sometimes painful, and expensive because it requires more of us. A hard pivot can kickstart courage. It helped me lay it all on the line and get honest with God. I was tired of the pretension and getting nowhere. It all aided in the crucial first step to growth: humility. I needed it to be open to the wisdom of God.

One of the marvels of spiritual growth is the realization that God has grace and mercy waiting for each hard decision and painful pivot. Grace is like a motor and helps us move from our thinking to His. This is exactly what I experienced. It was clear, He sensed my disappointment in life. Mercy invited me into His plan for living. When I answered that call and quieted my life, the discovery of strength through prayer and meditation was like a treasure map for life, and I couldn't get to the "X" fast enough. I just wanted to find the mother lode of peace and fulfillment.

Months passed, and I remained focused on His love. He helped me calm down and trust the process. I began to find grace for growth, a term I would repeat a dozen times a month that first year. Grace helped me choose the road of wisdom and walk it out. The funny thing about wisdom is, the more you gain, the more you long for wisdom. It became clear I needed more of it. The Bible says that God created the world with wisdom. Proverbs 3:19. He gives wisdom to anyone who asks for it. James 1:5. It became my daily request in prayer.

In that season of surrender, I sensed divine words that felt like whispers in my heart—words of wisdom to help me find peace. A new ability to see the potential of wisdom developed within me. Each concept inspired by wisdom is one brick that would help me build my life. These blocks were the four words that I affectionately refer to as the magic words of my life. Of course, they are not magic but gifts of wisdom. God's wisdom brought me from the ashes into a beautiful place of peace.

The Process

The process is the space between here and the dream. It's the path every person must journey to reach a fully mature, excellent soul. When I imagined my goal-line self, the word *Faithful* is strung across the finish line. It's part of my prized ideal. Maybe it's inspired by the verse in Matthew 25:23, imagining myself meeting God face-to-face, hearing Him say, *"Well done, good and faithful servant…"*

Maybe it was the realization that my character was stuck in reaction mode. I knew the only way to reach that dream was to commit to the process of maturity. Only God could develop that deep inner strength in me—the ability to be steady, loving, and faithful regardless of what was happening around me. It would require shifting my attention to the inner work of building myself instead of spinning plates. As I embarked on the journey, I began to realize I had been neglecting my inner world while obsessing over ladder climbing and prize hoarding. I had to stop chasing rainbows and build my inner world.

We possess an inner knowing. That internal message knows there's a higher being and a divine truth, higher than human rationale. Reading the Bible pours light into the depths of our souls and stimulates growth. God created us in His image and intended for us to know His thoughts and grow from them. He created and redeemed us to be loving, kind, noble, and faithful. Something in us knows we are noble by birth. The question is, will we go to God for this life force of dignity, love, and loyalty? Will we agree with His wisdom and live by it? Or will we hustle for a lesser version, so we can go our own way?

Resilient, unwavering faithfulness results from a sustained life sourced from spiritual love and wisdom. Truth be told, if we could make ourselves faithful, the cross and the work of Christ was unnecessary. Deep within, I recognized that true faithfulness went far beyond pious duty or robotic loyalty. I knew there was more. But what? How could I discover the truth?

What does it take to move from a hustle-driven lifestyle to one centered on the deep power of love that could not be shaken?

In order to develop the process, we have to be honest with ourselves. What are our current attitudes and patterns? Then we need to look into that deep well of wisdom from God and draw out His precepts for living in the light. A life of peace begins with agreement with the wisdom of God and adapting to it. The process.

Prayer and Meditation

This is how God led me through the process of healing and strength. It's how I built my life - and continue to build. As I share my story, consider how these inspirations could strengthen your soul and build your story. Even if it's not your current practice, pray before reading each chapter.

Quiet yourself. Open your expectations. Invite God to guide you through the process. We are all continuing to venture onto this mountain called life. Whether you are merely searching for spiritual clarity or have been navigating this road for decades and have the summit in sight, be open to more. Be willing to grow.

Where are you limiting God? Where are you making excuses for yourself or blaming others for your rut? Blame is not an excuse slip; it's a ditch. Only you can get yourself out of that ditch. The process demands that ditches be filled with grace. Don't limit your future by surrendering to your past.

Read God's wisdom about grace and mercy and let it reform your soul, releasing you from shame and inspiring you to release others. This book is about my transformation, and I wrote it to inspire yours! As your mind processes thoughts and inspirations, your heart is gathering ideas for the construction project of your life. Write them down! Figure them out later. Each reflective thought of hope, forgiveness, and wisdom is one more brick in the edifice of you.

The process is the path to wisdom. The longer we focus on wisdom, the clearer things become. Wisdom has a way of stirring courage and lighting up the next step, and it just keeps gaining strength. It's like working out at the gym. Strength is gained incrementally. God will give you more and more understanding of His love and reveal the power of His promises. He will calm your fears as you focus on the truth. He will win your heart and convince you—you are loved and He is faithful. As you spend time in prayer and meditation, you will sense Him working!

Action Steps

1. Commit to the Process: Build You, Daily

Continue with your daily time of prayer, reading, and reflection. Ask yourself: Am I chasing fantasy over growth?
- Write down insights and shifts in your thinking.
- *"It's a building plan, not a fairy tale. Transformation happens as we exchange our thinking for God's."*

2. Pursue Wisdom Intentionally

Make wisdom a daily pursuit—not a random hope.
- Commit to this simple prayer from James 1:5: *"God, I ask for Your wisdom today."*
- Read scripture and meditate on how it applies to your current challenges or choices.
- Practice delaying impulse-based decisions until you've sought wisdom and wise counsel. Proverbs 24:6.

3. Live From Love, Not For Love

Be aware of any performance patterns. Begin practicing the from love, not for love principle.

Reflect: "Where in my life am I hustling for love instead of living from love?"

- Reorient those actions to come from a place of peace, identity, and divine purpose—not fear or striving.

Faithfulness is not a badge earned by doing. It is the full maturity of love.

Addressing the Deep

What will bring our lives to a state of true peace? God holds the answer. Each one of us is unique in hunger, frustrations, thirst, and needs. God knows each one and how to satisfy our lives completely. Time spent in silent reflection, prayer, and meditation—focusing on and pondering wisdom, love, and peace—will transform us. This time of quiet each day allows our souls to calibrate to God's wisdom and grace. He knows exactly what we need and has hidden it within the Bible. Quiet meditation on the scriptures speaks volumes and inspires worship.

God knows how to address the emptiness, the questions, and the chaos. He will lead us to peace. This type of living requires us to turn off the screens and the reels of anger or complaints looping in our minds concerning the past, our parents, our kids, our work, or school, where fires are blazing. It requires us to quiet our surroundings and center our souls.

God created us to live in the light and broadcast it to the

world, living from the inside out. We don't ignore life, but we must have a center point that we tend to, where we find the clarity and peace to anchor ourselves. Only then can we bring any solution or help to others.

While you read these pages and later, as you practice the discipline of solitude, reading and praying as your daily practice, bring it all to a stop. Turn your eyes off what hurts, the storm that rages, the bills you can't pay, the diagnosis you can't solve, the person you can't change, and the puzzle of the past. The circumstances are a distraction from the work God wants to do within you. He will help tend to those things when the inner work has been done.

Soul first. If there's something for you to do, He will make it clear in the place of peace. Turn away from those distractions and build yourself. Look to Jesus and unload it all. Focus only on what He has done to save you. Focus on His work to heal your soul and redeem your peace. He is working from the inside for now. The outside will line up later. First things first —inner peace.

We have two grand purposes: to know and love God and to carry His light in the world. When we commit to these two primary callings, we discover ourselves. God is love, and He is light. The whole point of Christ's coming to Earth was to redeem us and lead us into the light, where we know the Father and discover our true nature: love and light. Our noble purpose and deepest sense of fulfillment will involve the same calling as Christ. Read that again.

The Father created and redeemed us into His Kingdom; now, our purpose is to act and speak as He does, fulfilling His will on Earth as it is in Heaven. Times of prayer and meditation on His Word will calibrate that deep calling and draw us into that space, filling us with peace so that we can carry peace to the world.

Healing from the Inside Out

Each of us will face storms: loss, disappointment, depression, hardship, loneliness, betrayal, disillusionment, lack, and fear. These are part of the human experience. Yet, in each of those dark valleys, we can rise above the circumstances by setting our hearts on the truth that outlasts temporary experiences. Our hunger for life is an echo of God's desire to create a divine version of life within humanity. He longs to bring elements of Heaven to Earth. Genesis reveals this in His choice to make us in His image. In Hebrews chapter eight, we read that the

Tabernacle is a pattern of the heavenly realm. This is truly a wonder, and we need to keep it in mind when we read the wisdom of God within the Bible. He intends to make our lives like Heaven on Earth. Jesus, God's only Son and our Redeemer, instructed us to pray for God's will to be done on Earth as it is in Heaven. Matthew 6:10 Our deep hunger for peace and joy is a divine echo of God's desire. Follow that echo. Silence the foolishness that rages against God's plan and agree with God. The result is heaven on earth.

Keep searching for the next gift of wisdom while celebrating the gifts within today. My forties decade motto: "Never settle for being an expert; when you could live as an explorer." He created us to be creative, innovative, and adventurous. He redeemed us to live in an amazing, continually expanding experience of life. Let His wonder break you free from the temptation to settle, park, and plateau.

When you feel like going your own way and fighting God's wisdom, pause and let Him bring the courage to take that hard pivot toward His wisdom. Wrestle toward God, not away from Him! Your life will expand if you explore.

Action Steps

1. **Continue in a Daily Quiet Time:**

What is something that inspired you in this chapter or at some point this week? Use those inspirations as prayer guides and ask God for wisdom concerning that seed of understanding.

2. **Meditate on the Wisdom That Builds Your Core:**

Write down a couple of inspirations from the Bible concerning who God says you are: Child of God, blessed, etc. (If you're not sure, look up Bible verses that define your value.)

3. **Practice "Wrestling Toward God":**

When doubts, frustrations, or questions arise, choose to lean into them as opportunities for spiritual growth instead of retreating. Ask God for clarity and peace, trusting Him to lead you to deeper understanding and strength.

Humble

Life is a mystery that can be ignored or explored! Within every mystery, there are secrets to discover. One potential gift of aging is perspective—a unique ability to see through a scope gained in exploration. Humility is essential on this quest. If we lean into the power of humility, knowledge and understanding add up. Before you know it, mysterious things emerge from the clouds and form wisdom. Time and grace reveal secrets. In truth, age is not required to obtain this vision. Humility is the doorway to wisdom, and it welcomes every guest, young and old.

Humility brings grace. Grace gifts us with a deep calm for issues that once perplexed us. It steadies us so that we can see with increased clarity. We learn how to navigate life with humility, wisdom, and grace, leading the way. Our road may be a long, narrow path, straight across the open plains, with mystery hidden in the hip-tall grassy greens of life. It may be a series of switchbacks, leading upward to a summit, hidden beyond the clouds.

No matter what defines our path, humility feeds wisdom, grace steadies our steps, and sets our vision. Humility is the birthplace of hope.

There's something quieting about humility. It settles us into knowledge and understanding. Humility reveals matters that exist outside opinions and experiences. It leads us to the truth. God is real, and there is wisdom high above our own. Humility leads us to this understanding. It comforts us to discover the goodness of God and His promise of shared wisdom. The quiet place and the promise of wisdom fill us with hope. The light of hope changes everything. We cannot thrive in life without it!

Wisdom holds the lantern. The longer we ponder our lives in that light, the more hope points our attention to the invisible moments when God was present throughout our history. Pondering this reality, we see the truth: He has always been with us, ready to reveal Himself and His goodness. Humility frees us from fault-finding and the negative thoughts we've accumulated. Hope loves to pull out the slideshow, the highlight reels of life, displaying the good times and blessings of life. Negativity holds the mic too long and dominates the average heart.

If we want to live a peaceful, fulfilled life, we need to discipline our souls and let hope have center stage. Hope takes over when we surrender old patterns for the higher ones God has in mind. Humility is the choice to sit in that space, listening to and agreeing with God.

As we take the time to meditate, humbly considering the goodness of God—focusing on not only His existence but His goodness and blessing—humility rises within us like the morning sun. It opens our hearts to see, remember the good, and to enjoy it. Humility is a beautiful door-opener, like the word *please*. It opens us to profound hope. This hope leads us to gratitude.

Sit in gratitude for long, and something intimate happens between your heart and God's. Something emerges from that quiet place. Quiet and humble, gratitude floods in like the dawn. As we turn our attention to God's goodness, the clouds of cynicism clear away. The fear that eclipses clarity and understanding melts away. This practice tunes our souls to resonate with hope, which has a song all its own. Hope sings in the depths of our souls. The lyrics remind us that God has always been present and has gifted us with people, moments, and blessings, enriching our lives.

Faith rises like the swell of a symphony when we realize He is doing something wonderful right now! He is always actively working, shining endless rays of goodness into our lives. When we decide to focus upward, we hear that divine melody; we see and enjoy these gifts. It's a focus issue. When anxiety and trouble blur our vision, we need to address what's distracting our souls.

Pain distorts vision. It can harden us. If you have experienced a series of losses, counting God's long list of blessings is difficult—and that's normal. Loss is part of life. Loss creates a vacuum that demands healing. Every one of us faces deep sorrow, and we need to address the consequent need for inner healing. You need a time of mourning to grieve the loss. Prayer is essential in this process. It allows God to maximize the exhale of grief.

People understand the principle of deep breathing to regulate the body during stress and anxiety. Prayer assists the soul in a similar exercise. Releasing sorrow to God eliminates the toxins of pain and creates a space for His compassion. He will help release the sorrow and receive healing. Exhale, inhale.

Ask God to lead you in the process from grieving to peace.

He will walk with you through the release and give you the next breath of hope. Journey that process with Him. Humility helps us navigate every journey and adjust our focus so we can find this joy.

Though the chapter is about humility, there is a benefit to humility that you may have already detected in the paragraphs above: **hope**. Humility is the spiritual alignment of our lives with the goodness of God. His goodness is so real, so powerful—it fills us with hope. Although it's not one of the magic words on my list, it's a bonus of the process.

The Bible refers to Him as the ***God of all hope***. That's a lot of hope—more than we will ever use in a lifetime. Humility leads to an unshakable level of hope. We need hope! It's a powerful thing! Hope heals our perception and gives us the ability to see the past through optimistic eyes. It enables us to see the future and the potential ahead.

Hope not only heals vision for the future but soothes the soul from the anxieties of the past. In the light of hope, renewed peace allows our muscles to loosen, shoulders to drop, heart rates to calm, and mental pressure to melt away.

God is with us. He is our ever-present help and hope. The more we humble ourselves to this truth, believing what He promised to be real, the more we find ourselves affected, spiritually rooted in hope.

God is with us, and His power changes us, filling us with His strength. God's power is real. The force of light and life He carries drives out the darkness. *"The hills melt like wax in the presence of the Lord."* (Psalm 97:5).

God is with us. We all face moments of fear. In those moments, recall this: **feelings reflect our focus, not reality**. When we focus on His promise, reminded that He is with us, that change in focus creates a change in feelings. When our focus shifts, our feelings follow. The more we focus on the goodness of God and His loyalty to watch over and care for us, the more we realize that there is nothing to fear. What began as a promise becomes a belief. God will prove His faithfulness. His protection and provision are eternal promises. His promise is the source of soul strength.

Here's the thing: the promise was true before our agreement. Humility leads us to believe in God when our feelings are contrary. It teaches us to align our thoughts, beliefs, and feelings, and to say *yes* to God's perspective. When we endure the process of surrender and commit to listening to and agreeing with God, we grow in character. That's a matter of deep inner strength.

The goodness that streams from that one decision impacts every area of our lives, especially mental health and spiritual wellness. God's wisdom affects every aspect of us. It goes to work shaping our thinking, inspiring better decisions, and transforming our nature. One of the most unexpected benefits I noticed in all these changes was a significant rise in self-respect.

Character is not only something that benefits society; it feels good privately and personally. It means you trust and respect yourself. But this only happens when we surrender childish patterns and commit to the wisdom of God. Maturity results from the painful process of agreement. The shift from selfishness to God-centeredness is not for the faint of heart. What I often tell those I mentor is this: God is real, whether we believe or not. Believing in and agreeing with God doesn't change His existence. It changes ours.

Reality exists without our agreement or acknowledgment. Better said: God exists with or without our consent.

Our feelings reveal our focus. When fear is rising, adjust your focus. Look away from what distracts you—to Jesus. See Hebrews 12:2. We plant faith, confidence, and courage within ourselves as we focus on God, the source of great power and hope. Setting our frame of mind on Him reshapes our experience of life. God is with us. He promises never to leave. Hope for today and tomorrow is our reality. He is undeniably, eternally present—yesterday, today, and forever. See Hebrews 13:8.

We can build our lives on this solid foundation of truth. Those who build their lives on the rock of faith in Christ will stand strong in the storms of life.

I realize that's a lot of focus on spiritual stuff, but to raise the roof, we have to create a solid foundation. That's a spirit-level matter. We function, think, speak, and live from the core level. I'm sure you've witnessed yourself saying one thing and doing another. You've seen that in others as well. Why? We often speak from the top of our heads, but we always move from the core of our being. Our core is the true GPS of our lives, and that's a spiritual matter.

Humility expedites spiritual wellness. It's where it all begins. The Bible tells us that humility is the starting place of wisdom.

Proverbs 11:2. I like to call it the door to all virtues—the key that unlocks the potential of life. Humility grants us access to a vantage point beyond all previous experience. There is no single event with wisdom. It requires continual surrender, day after day, choosing humility over prideful self-will. Humility draws us upward every day, lifting us to new heights. Each step of meekness leads us forward and up into wisdom.

God gives a mystical invitation: *"Call Me, and I will answer. I will show you mysteries you do not know."* Jeremiah 33:3 One Bible translation calls it hidden things. Have you ever been in a tough spot and said to yourself, "I'm clueless! I don't know what to do!" We've all been in that position. Our knowledge is limited, and sometimes those limitations show up when we need clarity the most.

Unfortunately, the pressing need for wisdom often accompanies a feeling of time pressure. We need the answer *now*. Humility moves at a different pace than worry. These are the perfect moments to access this promise and focus on God. Slowing our pace to the rhythm of humility is an investment program that pays off big! Urgency is always looking for slaves. Humility brings freedom and honor, rewarding us with wisdom and peace.

Worry makes us trigger-happy and willing to risk it all for the fleeting delusion of escape.

Humble yourself. Be calm. Slow down, pray, and listen. Wisdom is on the way. Wisdom will help you make decisions that will add long-term strength and peace.

God created the world with wisdom. He offers this wisdom to us. Divine intelligence is available to guide us through life's darkest hours. If we humble ourselves, wait, and listen for divine wisdom, He will give it to us. I know! It boggles my mind, too! Countless passages in the Bible relay this promise. Proverbs 25:2, one of my favorite passages, says that it glorifies God to conceal a matter and "it is to the glory of kings to search it out." Seriously! Pause and read that at least once more.

The wisdom you need for the next big deal in life is available. God has it tucked away and waiting, but you will have to slow down, make space, and be quiet to listen—honoring this divine setup that honors God as our source. Go ahead, read that verse again! When we live with humility in life, humility honors us. It raises us up into the best versions of ourselves. Humility is an ennobling virtue, turning us into kings.

We have wisdom from God to build our lives! What a promise! This is His promise to us. Take it! Choose this path of wisdom. Put your stake in the ground.

Live adventurously, guided by this divine gift. Humble yourself to hear His voice. He is speaking, giving hope for the journey. If your current path feels like a long, endless trek to nowhere, stop! Find a quiet space each morning and throughout the day. Make the time to search for wisdom. God will secure your steps and assure your heart. Navigating with God will make the path clear. He has promised His help to the humble. Luke 14:11 says God will lift those who humble themselves.

The Bible is a spiritual floodlight on the path leading us forward. Put your problem on the table in prayer, ask God for wisdom, dig into the Bible, and shine it on your decisions—your steps. Read Psalm 119:105 & Psalm 32:8. Reflect on the hopeful, peaceful thoughts you have gathered so far. God is speaking, whispering wisdom all day. Write it down and rehearse it in these moments of quiet. Build. Use the gathered wisdom and build new foundations of hope.

Humility provides much more than just wisdom. It affects our entire being. Humility will calm our mental state. Our experience of life and how we remember it is a matter of a chosen focus. Everyone has faced tragedy, and everyone has had sunshine and laughter. Which one defines our lives? That's a choice. You choose the photos for your highlight reel.

You choose the events that define your character and your life. Don't fall into the normal ditch of negativity. Choose the better way. Be sober-minded about your focus and how you define your life.

A negative mindset is a choice. First, we learn it as we mimic our models in life. But as adults, our patterns are a matter of choice. We can remain in the negative pattern or choose a new one—a better one. God is present to lift our heads from the ditch and show us the high road. When we live ignorant or deluded, blind and unaware of God's presence and promise, we live the lifestyle of a ditch-digger. Every stress feels like ours to feel and fix. Oh, I sure know that lifestyle. I lived for decades in that ditch. Just writing this paragraph was like the History Channel for me. Thank God for the saving power of His love! His love gave me the courage to surrender, and when I did, I could finally see the light.

If surrender feels impossible right now, meditate for the next few days on the immensity of His love for you. Love gives us the courage to believe. Surrender is the only way we will discover the power of humility.

Wisdom is the divine tool to lead us to strength. We don't lean on our understanding; we lean on His wisdom.

Humility reminds us of this and aids our broken thinking patterns, easing our stress, as we learn how to offload the weight of worry.

Worry doesn't change things. It has no intelligence. It is a massive distraction, a swirling cloud of fear. Humility guides us back to the pause, the pivot, the prayer that points us to the Person of God and the promise of His goodness. The Holy Spirit is the ultimate life coach. He embodies humility.

The Holy Spirit is here to help us. Like Christ, who rescued us, God gave the Holy Spirit to teach and empower us to live life to the fullest. His role on Earth is to guide and point to the Father.

In Proverbs 29:18, we read that where there is no vision, no redemptive revelation from God, the people perish. When we live a lifestyle of humility, open to the guidance of God, we live open to the redeeming voice of His wisdom. Wisdom is a course-correction device that directs us onto a path of peace and keeps us moving in the right direction. Love redeems the wandering steps we take in ignorance, anger, or pride. Wisdom points in the direction leading to peace.

God's wisdom is available to anyone who looks to Him with a humble heart, accepting who He is and the wisdom of His ways. Humility opens us to see, think, and live a better life, with new thoughts and attitudes. That same Bible verse in Proverbs wraps up by stating that whoever follows God's wisdom lives a happier life. "Blessed is the one who heeds wisdom's instruction". Wisdom leads us to the goodness of God. It may seem overly simplistic, but that's the way it is. Simple. Humility is the doorway to wisdom. Wisdom leads to peace, and our souls long for peace.

Action Steps

1. **Calibrate during Morning Reflections**
   Make your quiet place to pray, meditate, or journal happen day by day. Ask God to help you see through His eyes. Reflect on His goodness and surrender your worries.

2. **Bring your new setting to your day. Replace Reaction with Reflection**
   When conflict or confusion arises, pause before responding. Take a breath, humble your heart, and pray for wisdom. Humility often requires silence before clarity. Let grace inform your decisions.

Agreement with God

I love being a life coach, but I know my place. I'm one of many assistants in this generation — not the head coach. I endeavor to echo the voice of the Holy Spirit, adding wisdom and love to the lives of others. This is my role as the leader of my team and of those I influence in life. When I'm in the groove and functioning well, my message of hope should be what God is already whispering. God invites everyone on Earth to come and discover His thoughts for life.

We will never feel more alive than when we are walking in a lifestyle of love and wisdom, as He designed. It becomes an overflowing experience as we partner with God. God compels us to share His love with others. Something in us feels aligned when we say what He says and live generously as He models. That's what an echo is: a softer, exact reverb of the original voice. This is by far the highest experience in life — to bring encouragement to the lives of others, echoing the love of God.

Humility helps us to hear His voice, receive His healing, and agree with Him, aligning our minds with His wisdom.

Love compels us to echo that message of hope. It's the ultimate. When we're in pain and want healing for ourselves, we turn to God. We think healing is the entire point, but it's just the beginning. Healing is not the final destination, but the first step into the adventure of hope. The result of full healing is strength. Strength has a higher purpose. In the words of Eugene Peterson in The Message translation of the Bible, "Strength is for service, not for status."

Humility invites us into the process of healing and empowerment. There is often an invisible battle that rages against our choice of humility. It's like a chord or chain holding us to our past and perceptions. We resist humility as if it threatens our safety. We put God in a box based on our previous experience or filtered by the reputation of those who called themselves Christians but represented Him poorly.

Prejudice is a real thing. Most people carry a prejudice against God and keep Him in that little box. In those moments when you sense the urge to resist the idea of God's existence or goodness, ask yourself: Am I carrying some prejudices? Have I put God in a little box?

Humility is the key to letting God be God. It's also the key to lifting the lid off the box we've been living in.

Humility heals the mind, calms the neurocycles of our being, and creates an atmosphere within our body for restoration.

The Bible said what science is discovering today. 3 John 1:2 says, *I pray you may prosper in all things and be in health, just as your soul prospers.* In the Amplified, it says: *Beloved, I pray that in every way you may succeed and prosper and be in good health, just as your soul prospers.* The peace that we long for is part of God's redeeming plan and begins in the soul.

When we agree with God, His peace transforms our souls as we read and meditate on it. His wisdom contains regenerating power, renewing mental health, and bringing peace into our paradigms. Healthy mind, healthy life. James 1:8 says a person whose mind is all over the place is unstable in every matter of life. They are uncertain about everything they think, feel, or decide.

Humility leads us to look to God, who gives us a steady, clear, peaceful mind. All we have to do is ask. David said it this way: Psalm 86:11 *Give me an undivided heart that I may fear your name.*

Some people might question the word *fear*. It may trigger a knee-jerk reaction to hide or create space, distancing ourselves from God. David wasn't talking about that type of fear.

Our scope of the word is very limited. Our modern definition of fear refers to the state of being afraid, an appropriate response to danger. When the Old Testament was written, fear had a broader meaning, including a response of honor and reverence. To fear the Lord was to recognize and respond appropriately to His holy nature. Awe is appropriate for the King of all kings.

If we believe that God is anything but who He says He is — love, good, healer, provider — we will live at a distance. We will see a distorted view of reality. Fear contorts reality. But if we humble ourselves and hear these truths concerning who He is, faith will rise within us. A study of the names of God will reveal more or who He is and the goodness He intends for us. The more we know Him, the more our faith expands. Faith cultivates wisdom — and the building begins.

The reshaping of our lens is a process. Ask the Holy Spirit to help you see the goodness of God. The book of Isaiah (9:6) describes the Messiah with these comforting titles: *His name will be called Wonderful, Counselor, Mighty God, Everlasting Father, and Prince of Peace.* None of these descriptors of His nature should render a negative frame of fear, but holy awe, realizing the God of the universe made us His children. The Everlasting Father inspires awe and reverence. The Prince of Peace is not requesting us to approach Him afraid — quite the contrary.

Humility leads us to the Eden state of existence, known only by Adam and Eve, who walked with God every day. This state of peace can be our daily experience as we begin each day meditating on God's love and wisdom, calibrating our souls to peace. In this secret place of prayer, we are filled with peace. We carry that healing power into our homes and workplaces. God's original intention was for His fullness to fill us, so that we would love and care for others.

Consider humility's purpose. It opens us to connect with God. The shift from selfishness to humility is a powerful pivot. Early in life, we live from patterns of self-focus. It feels like a necessary mindset to ensure our safety. Putting myself first promises security. However, as time passes and the cost of selfishness increases. A journey lacking love and wisdom impoverishes the soul. If left unchecked, it will become our demise. To deny ourselves and follow Christ is the invitation from heaven. Here's the wonder, the mystery of this experience: when we deny ourselves, we become safer than ever.

We enter a place of discovery. Step by step, we discover the truth: God created us in His image, and He redeemed us to be His children. Humility reveals divine dignity. He paid a high price to redeem us and is committed to our growth. He has even arranged a personal trainer beyond Olympic standards to develop us to our full potential. The Holy Spirit echoes the wisdom of the Word, develops our character, and leads us in strength.

No earthly attempt at fulfillment can compare to what happens within us when the Spirit takes the lead. Psalm 16:11 *In Your presence is fullness of joy, and at Your side are pleasures forevermore.* Nothing holds a candle to God's level of goodness, which never fades away.

Humility leads to this wonderland and feeds us more and more of Heaven. Humility is the portal between heaven and earth. *Guide me on Your path so that light floods my daily walk.* Psalm 86:11

Where are you in this process? Locate yourself.

Think of the GPS in your vehicle. As you set off on a journey, you enter the address of your target destination. You find where you are and where you want to be. Only then can you find the path forward. Considering this illustration and locate yourself.

Don't let fear silence the truth. Be honest with God about where you feel stuck, what feels broken, and the lies or accusations that have imprisoned you. This is where you currently live. Be honest. Then, let God be honest. Ask Him to tell you the truth about grace and mercy. Let them be your rescue team. Let God be God. Don't make a bigger deal of your mess, as if it's greater than His grace. It's not. Accept grace as the superpower saving agent of all time. Grace is the first step toward peace. Prepare to pivot.

If shame, bitterness, or any other voice from the past questions why you are on track with Jesus, hold up that first-class ticket to peace that grace gave you. Don't let it go. Humility will be helpful here. Humility is your agreement with God, who redeemed you through Christ. Humility honors that gift and says yes to God.

As I mentioned at the beginning, when my journey began, I was wrestling with God and everyone else. I felt lost. I was a Christian, a leader in the church, had created an online mentoring website, and was leading others, but felt lost in my soul. I had taken the wrong road and was living far from peace.

Fear tormented me. Insecurity plagued me. Even though I looked like I had it all together, I teetered on the edge of infidelity for years, feeling hopeless about myself and my marriage. I was privately miserable, feeling worthless and unloved. When I located myself and was honest with God, we could finally get started on my relocation from chaos to peace.

Now it's your turn. What are the dominating thoughts guiding you at the core level? Be honest. Write them down. Look at them. Leave space on the page of your journal to process and add thoughts later. This may take weeks or even months to uncover. Take the time to unearth the roots of your sorrow or anger. You may need a therapist to help with this process. That's fine, but be sure to include God in your healing process.

Understanding our present position is the initial step toward change. Humility needs honesty to thrive. Every rooted, warped thought crippling us exists in the dark. Honesty allows us to deal with root issues and removes the weeds that choke out our hope. We can remove exposed lies and replace them with truthful, hopeful, and courageous thoughts. These new thoughts become the attitudes that shape our souls and reform our entire experience of life.

The practice of humility looks like this: it is replacing all the thoughts born in the dark with the light of God's goodness and love. Every crippling thought is rooted in darkness, fear, and doubt. But the light of God's Word brings light and understanding. Psalm 119:130 says, *The entrance of Your words gives light; it gives understanding to the simple.* This process delivers us from darkness to light.

What thoughts bring pain to your life? Be aware of them. Objectify them. See them separate from yourself. Those thoughts are ideas — separate from you. You may have allowed them inside, allowing them to define you for decades, but they don't have to be permanent restraints. They are thoughts you have lived by, and they are subject to change.

You can replace thoughts that others gave you, and you adopted, just as you would replace batteries in one of your devices. When the old batteries aren't serving you, what do you do? You replace them. Thoughts are the same. Beliefs are anchor thoughts. If they do not agree with God's definition of dignity and hope, they need to be replaced. Somebody sold you some dead batteries. God has new ones to empower you.

God invites us to live by His thoughts. The Bible says, *Let the wicked person forsake his thoughts. Wicked* means twisted and broken. At some point, we have all experienced anxiety twisting our minds.

You may even feel shattered or broken after a heartbreaking loss through death or divorce, a breakup, a business failure, or a dream that died. Maybe a child has gone off track or ostracized you, or you lost a child to a tragic disease.

Many experiences in life can break our hearts. In these dark seasons, we often form definitions to create a sense of order in our souls. These definitions are usually fear-based, tainted tactics that promise protection. If not replaced with truth and hope, we become paralyzed by our paradigms. If you resonate with this, there is a healing source that will restore your soul. I know several people who have experienced the things listed. I have watched them tend to their souls and rise again with hope and peace.

We are pliable, redeemable, renewable creatures. You can become renewed. Your life can be redeemed and restored. It's a process, and we will have to learn how to use a healthy mind. When we turn away from our broken version, God will give us a fresh start and teach us how to function with that new mind.

Thoughts make a person from the inside out. When we allow ourselves to accept the fresh start God offers, He helps us develop a fresh perspective. Like every growth process, it's step by step. We renew our minds with each intentional choice, exchanging old thoughts for new ones. God's thoughts of wisdom and peace lift our lives into a better place.

Humility allows us to exchange our thoughts for God's. Pride resists, but humility runs to wisdom and dives in. It may be a dip-the-toe experience at first, but the payoff of wisdom is undeniable. We all love peace and joy. That's what wisdom delivers. Before long, we are running and diving in — no questions asked. God's thoughts are not ours. His thoughts are higher. Isaiah 55:8-9 His wisdom lifts us out of the ditch of old thinking. Dignity, justice, peace, and hope are just a few of the beautiful things we can expect when we choose humility and dive into the ocean of wisdom.

God invites us to think with Him. In the book of Revelation, God says, *Come up here.* Revelation 4:1 It may have been a revelation reserved for John, but this is the nature of God: to invite us to understanding. Baffling as it may seem, God is not a king who distances Himself, but the ultimate Father who wants us to feel the wonder of belonging. Christ came to show the Father's goodness and to be our bridge of hope. We often refer to Him simply as God, but He is a Tri-une being: the Father, the Son, and the Holy Spirit. He wants us to know Him as Father. This is the reason Christ came to earth — to reveal the Father and reconcile humanity to Him.

In knowing Him, we learn the truth of who we are. When we see Him, we see ourselves — not because we are God, but because He made us in His image. The only way we can find ourselves is by finding God through Jesus Christ. That is why He says, *Come up here.* God intended to make Himself known and to cohabitate with us in life. How can we know this? In the Garden of Eden, God walked with Adam and Eve each day. They drew on God's wisdom daily. He invites us into that lifestyle.

There is an ennobling purpose in humility. It doesn't lower us into some weak, pathetic rendition of ourselves. It transforms us as we surrender every selfish thought and attitude to live in the wisdom and love of God. There are many inspiring definitions of humility. In Rick Warren's culture-shaping book, The Purpose Drive Life, he shares an inspiring take on humility: Humility isn't "thinking less of yourself, but thinking of yourself less often." This is true, but there is a definition that I discovered in prayer that has surpassed all others: **Humility is agreement with God.** From that epicenter of virtue, all other expressions of humility spring to life.

Humility is the threshold we cross between human nature and the redeemed nature. It opens the door to every great virtue and the life for which we were created and redeemed. The picture I envision when defining humility is that agreement with God is the tree, and all expressions of humility are the flowers on that tree. When we see behaviors and call them humility, they are expressions of God's nature coming to life in and through us. Complete humility exists only in the soul surrendered in agreement with God.

No medal is given when we choose humility. No one may even notice at first. But Heaven does. Angels lean in. God responds. It's the secret door that opens to the fullness of life. Jesus modeled it, not just in His death, but in His way of life. His life was the truest echo of the Father. The more we agree with God, the more we begin to look like Christ.

Encouragement for Humility

Humility is not weakness. It's courage rooted in God. It's the decision to live in the light, one honest moment at a time. You will experience the peace, joy, and strength that come from walking in step with the One who made you. You were made to live free, and humility is the key to that freedom. It is the construction of character. The sculpture of the soul.

Our culture largely ignores this quest for character development, which is sad. For decades, I have heard wise people say talent may get you on the pedestal, but only character can keep you there. Humility is the key virtue of character. I may sound like a broken record, but this is a countercultural ideology. For many decades, the mantra of our nation has been that we are self-made. The Bible teaches differently: we did not create ourselves, and we are not the highest form of intelligence.

Humility invites us to embrace our Maker and to draw from His intelligence. We need to push against the undertow of culture into the virtues of the invisible, so we can discover the power of humility and the wonders of wisdom.

Humility will take us further than pride. It keeps us open to the ocean of wisdom. From now until our last day, there will always be mountains to conquer, lands to discover, mysteries to explore, and life to embrace. These adventures are the reward for the explorers. I don't have a tattoo, but if I did, one of my life mottos would be on my right arm: *Never settle for being an expert when you can live as an explorer!* Experts park at their discovery. Explorers consider each discovery as one more clue to keep climbing.

There is a natural hunger for more within the human soul. Sometimes, that never-enough feeling gets us into trouble. It can also help us, however, to live open to all that God has intended. God will use our humility and hunger as a pathway to more wisdom. The level of "more" available to us is something no human can define. There is a boundless wilderness of wisdom to explore. When we follow the Spirit, wonder will be our reward, silencing the never-enough hunger and satisfying it with God. When we humble ourselves, as the Christmas carol recites, *He satisfies our hunger with the wonders of His love* ("Joy to the World").

Locate yourself

Where have you been living up to this point? What thoughts have created and carved out the borders of your existence? How have you defined God, yourself, and others? What anxieties prevent you from pursuing your desires? Self-awareness is very helpful in discovering your current beliefs. Beliefs form the behavior that creates the habits which build our lives. When we reflect on our habits and the beliefs that form them, the root issues become evident. Those roots are the core beliefs we hold about ourselves, others, and God. We can change these core beliefs and reshape our lives.

God wants us to be rooted in love. Ephesians 3:17. Love drives out fear and creates positive, courageous thoughts, attitudes, and actions. 1 John 4:18. Love builds the heart of God into the lives of those who follow Him. Agreement with Him puts us into the strongest, healthiest state of being. The human bent, however, leans toward fear.

A fearful heart ruminates on the idea that God is not present, compassionate, or active in our lives. A prideful mindset may suggest that God either doesn't exist or is not interested in our lives. Locate yourself on the grid of these beliefs. The willingness to be honest with God is itself an expression of humility. He will honor your humility and graciously help you find the clarity of truth. Whether it's surrendering fear or pride, God will meet you where you are and gift you with grace for the next step forward.

You can live a life of peace and joy. It begins with righteousness—agreeing with God—and allowing Him to make all the broken and twisted places straight. He does the heavy lifting in this process. Mercy and grace are the superpower forces that lead us into this state of being. Righteousness, peace, and joy are His, the defining virtues of His culture, and, through humility, they become our reality and destiny.

Action Steps

1. **Consider something you don't fully understand.**

Ask God to reveal hidden wisdom. Look in the Bible for wisdom and understanding.

2. **Create a Hope Reel in your soul**

Make a list of highlights from your past that remind you of God's presence and goodness.

3. **Sit with Hope**

Make some time for stillness and meditate on God's promises. Let hope rise naturally from the quiet.

Grateful

The topic of gratitude has intrigued thinkers and writers throughout history. Countless quotes celebrate its significance. One of my favorites comes from the simple yet wise words of *VeggieTales'* Madame Blueberry, who reminds young and old that "a thankful heart is a happy heart." Greater still, the Bible points us to the mystical power of this virtue. When we choose gratitude, we find the sacred entrance into the presence of God. Only those who are thankful can enter the gates (Psalm 100:4). Humility is the gateway to all virtues, and gratitude is the path to awareness and the experience of God's presence.

Discontentment is a plague in our culture. For most of my life, it has defined my attitude and emotional climate. The "never enough" virus used to plague my soul. I would never have admitted it publicly. Discontentment is not a Christian virtue. However, nothing—not even myself—could ever bring me happiness. This cynical attitude robbed me of enjoying the blessings that were around me every day.

Not only was I plagued by discontentment, but I was also afraid that if I didn't do everything right, my kids would suffer. So I did everything I knew to make sure they would be safe and successful. Those dear kids were my project. I was trying to mold them into exceptional humans rather than just loving and enjoying them.

Almost daily, listening to audiotapes in the car or around the house was required of everyone. Before they entered adolescence, my kids knew the wisdom of Zig Ziglar, Jim Rohn, and John Maxwell. Before middle school, my girls were reading John Maxwell—required reading. The perpetual tension of my expectations was no fun to live with. I regret how long it took for me to realize the truth. Fear was driving my ambition and driving my family to resentment.

The only cure for all this fear was God's perfect love. Humility led me to that redeeming revelation. When I reached the end of my rope and agreed with God, humility opened my eyes and my heart. That was the starting point of my transformation, but I'm getting ahead of myself. Let me explain the process.

Much to my surprise, the first area God addressed was the belief that I was not worthy of love. It may seem odd that humility taught me my worth, but remember, humility is agreeing with God, who considered us worth dying for. Humility helped me stop fighting and start seeing God's perfect love. I knew God loved the world, but it's an enormous leap of faith to make it personal. When we realize His love is for us, individually as well as globally, we see differently. We realize that He is with us, ready to guide every step.

Hurdles of Pain

Yes, this chapter is on gratitude, but to get there, we have to see and deal with what keeps us from living in gratitude. Discontentment is one hurdle. Here's another: pain.

Earlier, I mentioned how pain forms lies and raises a frame of fear around our perspective. Unless those lies are confronted, we repeat the cycles that created the lies to begin with. In the Old Testament, a man named Jabez has a prayer that sheds some light on the subject of pain.

The story is unpacked in the famous mini-book *The Prayer of Jabez*, published in the 1990s by Dr. Bruce Wilkinson, which quotes a passage in Scripture filled with wisdom. In that prayer, Jabez makes a comment and a request, correlating sin and pain.

1 Chronicles 4:9-10: "…oh that Your hand would be with me and that You would keep me from evil, that I may not cause pain!"

What a window into the reality of pain cycles. Selfishness causes pain for everyone involved—including ourselves. When we maintain our lives with selfishness, we perpetuate the mindset and lifestyle that created the very pain we despise. Pain caused by others is repeated, unless we break the cycle. We can stop these pain cycles.

Humility can cease the cyclone of sin and rescue us from the avalanche. As we surrender our thoughts, exchanging them for the wisdom of God, we emerge from that crazy spin cycle. Humility leads us to love. Love breaks the chains created by fear. Gratitude reforms our thinking, and a brand-new life of peace becomes our norm. Ahhh, nothing compares to peace of mind.

If gratitude feels foreign or phony, there may be resentment lingering in your soul yet to be surrendered. Pain needs to be addressed. If you have experienced significant trauma, find a licensed therapist for this process. Return to that place of pain with someone who can guide you into healing.

We live in the invisible cycles formed by our experiences. The good news is that broken cycles can be healed and renewed. As we learn new patterns of thinking by agreeing with God for what defines our being and our purpose, we rise above the ashes of the past. Repeating the healing processes, exchanging our thoughts for His thoughts, is the path to renewal. It's like learning a new athletic skill. Learn the right form and repeat often, and you will transform your being. Bring your crisis, your challenge, addictions, anger, depression, pride, or whatever else is crushing your life - and release it to God. Ask Him for grace to see the truth and wisdom to rise above it.

Choose to move on and release yourself from the past, agreeing with God. Give yourself grace for growth.

Why is it so vitally important to practice the healing of these pain cycles? Simple. Our natural setting is selfishness. When we forgive all people, others, and ourselves, we can be released into the freedom God intends for us. This freedom opens our hearts to enjoy life. Gratitude rises from that wellspring of peace.

It doesn't have to be deep trauma. Low-grade cynacism from minor disappointments can mount up and create a mountain in our hearts. Humility will require us to lay our hang-ups down. What drags us down is what King Solomon calls **the little foxes.** Song of Solomon 2:15 Little habits of complaining, giving two cents to frustrating drivers on the road, eye-rolling, etc. When the little things are unattended, they become the leaky points in our lives.

These matters truly drain us slowly. They are like the little foxes in the vineyard that sneak around and spoil the harvest.

However, the simple choice to tend to those hurdles can create peace, happiness, and gratitude.

An Open Heart

Gratitude is the ability to see and enjoy the goodness of God and all the blessings within life. This goal of living so full and free that gratitude emerges like a fountain from our soul - now that's living! This is what God intended for us. It was declared at the birth of Christ. Peace on Earth—goodwill to men. Luke 2:14. It's a great headline for His intentions. That's what it's like to live by the wisdom and love of God—Peaceful.

That reality may seem like a phony fantasy compared to what you've known so far. But God's will is reality - not fantasy. Our lives may have been a broken road, but His path of life is real, and we are invited to walk it out into His dream for us.

Initially, my experience with changing paths was clunky. Fear had me like a puppet. It was going to be a slow, steady climb, but I was miserable and wanted a change. This discomfort would not stop me. My approach involved considering one thought at a time and replacing it with what I found in the Bible. During that stretch of the road, I would talk to myself during a battle of challenging mindsets. I would talk out loud so I could hear myself unpack what was going on within. When fear tried to dominate me, I would audibly say, "That's wrong. God is right." Plain and simple. Everything in me opposed the thoughts of dignity, peace, and confidence that were woven into the Gospel. Humility led me to agree with God until finally, I could see differently. Seeing became believing.

I cannot possibly estimate how many times I had to talk to myself like that, but that phrase helped me envision the exchange. Fear was wrong. Pride was wrong. Resentment was wrong. God was right. I trained my mindset to agree with Him. Repeating that phrase brought inner peace. God's thoughts provide us with the perfect plumb line to lift our lives. His thoughts of love and wisdom help us realize where we are living selfishly, fearfully, or in ignorance.

As I kept that clarifying phrase in my daily routine, I discovered something. I spoke a little less often. When I spoke, I gave more thought to the value I was bringing to others. I gave thought to what others were going through and how it's affecting them, creating new levels of empathy. I saved my thoughts until they became valuable. I learned how to pause and wait for wisdom before I spoke.

I'm still learning the power of the pause. Creating margins for our hearts to gather empathy and wait for wisdom is the mark of maturity. As I gave myself to this path, I realized people were trying their best, just like I was. My fuse became longer; patience was attainable. I viewed others with greater respect.

This was the world's largest intro to get to this point. Gratitude becomes a free-flowing, real flow of wonder and joy when we deal with all the garbage we've been collecting in life. Dealing with what hurts, enrages, paralizes, and prompts us to selfishness must be dealt with if we are going to have and enjoy this life. John 10:10 This is only possible by processing each hurdle with the wisdom and grace of God. Letting go of these issues sets us free to have and enjoy life and be filled with gratitude.

Action Steps

1. **Start a Daily Gratitude Practice**
   Every morning or evening, write down three specific things you're thankful for. Be consistent—even when it feels awkward or forced. This habit will reframe your mindset over time.

2. **Catch and Replace Negative Thoughts**
   When fear, discontentment, or resentment surface, pause and say aloud: *"That's wrong; God is right."* Use this as your reset point. Replace the thought with a biblical truth or promise.

3. **Tend to Your Inner Garden**
   Regularly check your heart for bitterness, judgment, or pride. If you notice these "little foxes," return to humility. Confess, release, and invite God's love to fill that space with peace and gratitude.

Gratitude for the Win

People often consider gratitude a feeling. I would like to suggest an addition: gratitude is a way of seeing. As I began this quest with God, with my marriage in danger and my family in pain, one of the first things God attended to was my vision issues. I was blind. I'm not saying there was nothing wrong with my relationship. My husband and I were relational babies. We lacked role models who had great communication and connection skills. We had very sweet parents, don't get me wrong. But sweetness is not a prerequisite for wisdom. Connection is a condition that happens with intentional thoughts and actions. We lacked those skills.

At the stage in the marriage where I was weighing out how damaging it would be to leave, considering the pain it would create in my kids and the chaos for all our relationships, I needed a God-sized plan. I had no idea how to make it better. What do you do in moments like that? I pray.

Months of prayers. Finally, God dropped the word "cherish" into my heart. I could feel it inside. It became like one of those neon lights in a city. Bright and clear. So I followed it. What did it mean?

I needed to cherish Kevin. I thought that was simple—just have warm thoughts, by choice. It was a good start, but God had a lesson prepared on what it meant to cherish. It turns out to be a very old word with a rich meaning. I dug into the history and origins of what it meant to cherish.

After a long trek of definitions and reading, I landed on the original word that preceded all the variations. It was more inspiring than simply warm thoughts. From the moment I found it, I knew everything was about to change, beginning with me. What was that word? *Prosdechomai*. I know—what? It's a Greek word that means to receive into oneself, accept someone favorably, to expect, look for, wait for.

Okay, I promise. That's the only Greek you will have to learn for the rest of the book. Now, to unpack it. When I first saw it, I could truly say, it's all Greek to me! I didn't understand how to cherish Kevin, in line with this definition. Over the next few days, I began to see the definition, like a virtual blueprint before my eyes, giving me the ability to see Kevin differently.

During prayer, I sensed God explaining it this way: Your problem is in how you see Kevin. I sensed Him unveiling how I perceived my husband:

"You see him through the filter of your unmet needs. Those needs are real. You are living a neglected life and feel starved and hurt. When you see him, you see your pain. You see him only through that lens. But here's the truth. Kevin has the potential to be a great person, a loving, attentive husband. There's potential in you as well. You haven't even scratched the surface of the woman I intend you to be. Both of you can continue in ignorance or learn, grow, and thrive in wisdom and love. Your choice. If you want to follow that second option, you need to understand how to function with *prosdechomai*— how to see, look forward, and expect favor. You need to see the gold in Kevin and believe now in who he is becoming."

Here's how I rephrased it for myself: start treating Kevin as if he were quickly becoming and striving to be that man, the one who is wise, loving, and attentive as a husband and father. None of my previous tactics of pouting or raging worked. God had something cool in mind. He told me what to do. I humbled myself—let's be real—initially because I was desperate. Eventually, I humbled myself and agreed with God because I could see it working. Humility works, even when we are half-hearted—thanks to God's grace.

I saw Kevin through new eyes. With *prosdechomai* as my new lens, I saw differently. When I treated him with more respect, he appreciated it and reciprocated. Gratitude went through the roof. Here's why. We often use gratitude looking backwards. We see what we appreciate and give thanks. With *prosdechomai* in action, I was now looking ahead at the good that was yet to come and giving Kevin credit for the future victories.

Not only is that a lesson in gratitude, but it's also a seed of faith. I realized that seeing him with expectation filled me with gratitude. I became increasingly thankful to be together. It changed the way I perceived him. I could see the good—not just in the future, but the good I had been overlooking in the present.

Gratitude is cherishing life's goodness—people, opportunities, and blessings—and fills our souls with gratitude. It allows us to see and enjoy it all. Bitterness eclipses the wonder of it all. Just like the moon that can black out the enormous sun, discontentment, unforgiveness, anger, hate, and rejection can block the light of hope and black out our lives.

Thank God there is a way back to the light. God will push those matters aside with one word. Humility aligns us with His wisdom. It opens our hearts to live in His grace. The eclipse is over. Gratitude is restored.

The learning curve of life goes on into eternity, but we can gain the seeds of grace and wisdom instantly. Grace and wisdom are available when we surrender ourselves to the all-powerful pause. Humility creates the margins needed for us to breathe and find clarity. In that space, God will work in us, enlarging our hearts and expanding our minds. What does this have to do with gratitude? Glad you asked!

Gratitude shapes our temperament. Impatience stems from fear. Fear tells us there is not enough, so we'd better hustle to ensure we get what we want and protect what's ours. Gratitude reminds us that God is here. He will forever be good to us. Gratitude, surprisingly, gives us the confidence to wait, to pause, to trust, and in that pause, great good happens. Bet you didn't think gratitude could do all that for you! Gratitude holds up the picture of God's goodness. That picture instills confidence. Those who wait, who have the power to pause, do so because they are confident of the good God has in store. We find strength in the margins. Isaiah 40:31.

Gratitude allows us to live with a different frame of mind. It stems from recognizing divine love as the source of all goodness. If we are infinitely loved to this degree, what is there to fear? Reflect upon life's gifts and the gift-giver.

Life is a gift. Loving, trustworthy friends and family are gifts. Consider yourself wealthy if you have more than a couple of dear hearts in your life. There is an old song I learned in my childhood: *Count Your Blessings*. We sang it often at our church and at home. There are countless gifts to inventory in life—experiences that bring laughter, joy, and wonder; health, strength, vision, food, water, and the ability to hear, etc. You determine the length of that list. When you enlarge the list, you enlarge your heart.

Gratitude is powerful, and those who turn toward it and welcome it into their lives enjoy life as God intended. Gratitude points the heart toward the giver of all good things. God fills the heart turned toward Him with hope, peace, and joy. Truly, every perfect gift comes from the Father of lights. James 1:17. Those who count those gifts fill their soul with light.

Living a life of joy begins with choosing the path of gratitude. Life presents constant choices. Training ourselves to react to those choices is part of maturity. It requires a certain level of autonomy. Many days, you may feel all alone on the narrow road of love, looking through the lens of gratitude for the next steps, not sure if your loved ones will join you. Use this time of solitude to refine your vision and enlarge your heart. Reflect on the best parts of your past. They happened! Don't let them get clouded over by resentment or sorrow. Don't allow those treasures to get ripped out of your memory because of the accusations and grudges of others. Look back for lessons, wisdom, and understanding that life has given you. Count your blessings, your wins, your favorites, and hold them dear. Silence and solitude can amplify gratitude in your soul. Time of meditation on what is good in life allows us to treasure what we've gathered in the past.

Consider organizing these thoughts into a gratitude journal, a history book of your life. Gratitude inspires; reflection confirms its power and allows us to stand with added strength. We gain wisdom and insight from reflection. We can walk into the future stronger with these gifts from the past.

Contemplation of lessons learned gives tremendous hope for the future. Don't leave the treasures of your life in the ruins of what went wrong. You have had countless beautiful moments, precious people, happy days, and gathered great wisdom. Go back and get it! Reclaim the riches of your history. Make it yours again. Be grateful! I bet you never expected all of that from that little thing called gratitude. It's a heaven-sized gift of perspective. God gives us all the tools needed to build a life of peace. He has given us the mind of Christ. 1 Corinthians 2:16. He invites us to enter His presence with thankful hearts. When we review our history through the lens of gratitude, we find many hidden gifts that feed our hope and happiness. That paradigm causes us to see the future through fresh eyes. We have courage while standing in the unknown.

How can we live this confidently? Because the nature of God is loyalty and generosity. He will never change. His goodness is our hope. His loyalty is our promise. The One who used heaven's wealth to make us rich spiritually has only started the good work. There is so much ahead to enjoy on earth and in heaven.

Gratitude. That's what captivates and compels me to live and give all I can to bless those on my path. Gratitude allows me the wonder of living off the goodness of the past. It fills me with anticipation of what's about to happen. It gives me unshakable hope in the days to come. Like the Proverbs 31 woman, I can laugh, with joyful expectation, at the days ahead —because I know the One who holds the future holds me. Make this your statement of faith.

He will never cease being good to us. Jeremiah 32:40. Gratitude reminds us of that truth. A grateful heart makes brave, bold choices. It inspires us to keep love as our key purpose, with no record of wrongs—just a long list in our Gratitude Journal.

Final Thoughts on Gratitude

Create a gratitude journal for one month, writing one detail daily that you experienced, enjoyed, and are thankful for. In his book, The Compound Effect, Darren Hardy shares how keeping a daily gratitude journal for one year transformed his perspective, marriage, and life. The journal he created was all about his daily observations and moments of thanks for his wife. He gave her the journal as a gift for the following Thanksgiving. Wow! What a practice and what a gift! Consider the goodness within your life. Feel, enjoy, and express gratitude for the people, things, and events that have brought joy and wonder. Write them down. This practice is powerful for centering and strengthening the soul.

Reflect on each entry and allow yourself to feel the significance of each gift. Allow yourself to pause and ponder the goodness. Enjoy it like a great meal.

Make gratitude appointments before each meal. Pause for thirty seconds before eating. Look at your food. Consider the blessing of that meal. Someone on the planet is not eating today. Be thankful. The old tradition of giving thanks before a meal has kept generations of hearts turning toward gratitude.

Remind yourself in the challenging times that there was good in your past; there will be good in your future. There is good where you are right now. Look for it, and you will find it, and when you do, focus on it.

"A thankful heart is a happy heart." —Madame Blueberry.

Action Steps

1. **Use the "Future Lens."**
   Each day, look at a loved one and speak words of encouragement as if they were becoming the best version of themselves. Cherish them *now* for who they are becoming.

2. **Begin a Gratitude Journal**
   Write down one detailed experience daily that you are thankful for—something seen, heard, or felt. Keep it simple, but consistent.

3. **Practice the Power of the Pause**

Before reacting in frustration or fear, take 30 seconds to breathe and remember one past moment of God's goodness. Let that shift your mindset before responding.

Noble

There's nothing like living out a dream. As I write this chapter, I'm doing just that—watching a dream come to life. For decades, I have quietly carried the hope of writing books that would bring encouragement to others. My husband has been prodding me for twenty-five years to take the leap. I know! Finally! I've been a writer since childhood. Over the last thirty years, I have devoted my writing to lullabies for my children, songs for our church, a seven-year online devotional series, and copywriting for my workplace.

Today, I am living a dream within a dream. As I planned out this project, my first published book, I knew the content of the chapters and reserved the writing session for this one for my favorite place on Earth. It doesn't get better than this!

Nestled beneath the alpine slope of the Rocky Mountains in Colorado sits the sacred sanctuary of St. Catherine's of the Rockies. I deeply cherish this chapel. Discovered at a moment of desperation in my life, it symbolizes healing, hope, and the rescuing love of God. I came here years ago after a brain stem injury—the cause of my third concussion. The damage was far worse than the previous concussions. Prolonged symptoms affected my thinking and emotional processes. My fragility and fear of the future, wondering if it included limited cognitive abilities, terrified me. As I unpack my soul and write the thoughts that make up this chapter, I am wrapped in wonder again, riveted by the beauty of this stone sanctuary.

Reliving the magic of that healing moment, contemplating the wonder that God loves humanity so much, I am savoring His love. He saves us continually. In a hundred ways, He saves us. This is where I will write about the power of His love and how it shapes our entire being, especially our identity. He builds us, like this chapel, into a holy, beautiful ambassador of hope.

During the healing process of that concussion, I visited one of my daughters in Colorado. Our family has a great love of the Rocky Mountains and has vacationed there for decades. Despite post-concussion and altitude-induced headaches, the beautiful skyline soothed my soul. During the trip, we took a route into Estes Park that I had never traveled before. There's nothing I love more than a new view of the Rockies.

Driving along the ribbon-curl roads toward town, I discovered the little gem of St. Catherine's. It is the most beautiful stone cathedral I have ever seen. The summit-sized accessories didn't hurt. The stone-crafted cathedral and the perfect snow-capped mountain backdrop were worthy of an epic feature film. It captivated me. I felt as if heaven had swept me away.

My daughter graciously changed her plans, making time for me to sit alone in the sanctuary for what felt like an eternity. It was only thirty minutes, but the fog of my brain injury and the wonder of St. Catherine's beauty made it all feel like a dream. The experience gifted me with a permanent imprint of wonder. I was overwhelmed—and that is an understatement.

Instead of running to the altar and falling on my face, I opted for a quieter option and plunked into the closest wooden pew. A deep sigh poured out of my lungs as I released the weight that had been crushing me. Resting in that little chapel, I silently unzipped my soul. I felt like an ultramarathon runner falling across the finish line.

The wash of relief rushing over me will never leave my memory. As my prayers fell like rain from my face, I sat in silence and wonder and waited for God. Fragile, frightened, and hopeless, I sat in the golden glow of the stained-glass sanctuary. I waited for God. I confessed how I felt, whispering a simple prayer for healing and hope. In this stone and stained-glass chapel, He answered. God spoke to me.

With words heard only in my soul, He communicated a message that calmed my mind as His perfect love washed over me. With a very real, tangible comfort, I felt showered in the promise of His healing and the hope of great good ahead. It was a powerful, spiritual, emotional experience. His words calmed the rugged waves of fear that had dominated me. A deep sense of knowing calmed the inner storm. His faithfulness was clear, and His promise was certain. I felt completely known, loved, and completely rescued.

He could have spoken anywhere, but He waited until I would look to Him in a place of profound beauty and wonder—in the middle of the mountains, one of my greatest loves. I love that! Every time I recall that moment, I am reminded that this is His nature. He wants us to know Him. He wants us to enjoy the comfort of being known and fully loved. There in the mountains, He assured me of His love and my future.

It's been three years since that transformational day. Seated back in the same sanctuary, I have returned to pen this chapter.

I returned out of deep gratitude and childlike faith to find more of His inspiration as I write words of hope and healing for others. This was the perfect place to write about the dignity God gifts to us.

As we dive into the subject of what it means to be noble and why it's so significant to becoming faithful, let's focus on the saint who is honored in this edifice. Who was St. Catherine?

Caterina Benincasa was born in Tuscany, Italy, in 1347. Her life was a series of wonders that led to her being canonized in 1461. She led a life of devotion to Christ, service to the poor, and carried a message of reform to the Church. Her bravery and devotion pointed many to Christ.

The title of saint is common in the Catholic Church but often reserved only for the exceptional, like St. Catherine. But the Bible refers to sainthood as the title and expected state for all believers, not a select few. Saints in the Bible refer to those who live fully committed to Christ.

There's something very important to consider in the title of saint and the subject of nobility. We need to soberly consider how God uses these descriptions and those He calls noble. When we agree with God and accept the divine dignity endowed to us, it changes the way we see ourselves, which determines the way we live our lives.

We are not sinners saved by grace, which is a human doctrine—not Scripture. We are who God says we are: dearly loved children of God, a new creation, saints, 1 Corinthians 1:2, crowned with honor. These are not sentiments of ego; they are titles revealing identity, character, and redeemed paradigms. We live from the well of our belief. Agreeing with God starts with humility and lifts us into a new identity. We receive righteousness. We become representatives of God—full of love, compassion, mercy, grace, and wisdom. Children of the King. Noble.

God created every human in His image, and by His breath, we live. Selfishness robs us of life and cripples us in what the Bible calls sin. Everyone who lives by that self-centered nature lives in sin and is dead spiritually. Humbling ourselves and honoring God, reconciling through Christ's redeeming work, leads to life. We receive new life, wisdom, grace, and so much more when we follow Christ. The life He died to give us is a mystical thing. He calls us to be servants of all, yet crowns us with honor, calling us kings and priests. Only through the humble pursuit of divine wisdom do we discover our created and redeemed purpose.

We discover true significance as we are reborn and adopted as God's children through Christ. Paul said it this way: "It's no longer I that live but Christ that lives in me." Galatians 2:20 He also redefines our nature, stating we are temples of the Holy Spirit, 1 Corinthians 6:19, vessels of honor, 2 Timothy 2:21. That's a mind-bender. The Bible says that in Christ, God has made us as righteous as Himself—holy. 2 Corinthians 5:21. To immerse ourselves in this truth, we have to return to the first point: humility is agreement with God. We cannot step into our redeemed identity without full surrender, which requires complete humility and agreement with God.

"How precious on the mountain are the feet of those who carry good news." Isaiah 52:7 When we surrender ourselves to Him, we are vessels, messengers, healers, preachers, and teachers of hope. We carry the Spirit of God, bringing His peace to humanity. As we bring compassion to the world, sharing the message of God's saving grace, bringing healing and hope to humanity, we are living examples of Christ. What a noble life!

Ephesians 3:19 says, *Be complete, filled, and flooded with God Himself.* He is not calling us to be reduced, but increased in our experience of strength, hope, and joy. Listen to the wording in Philippians 2:14-15 (paraphrased): *Do everything without complaining or arguing, so that you may be blameless and pure children of God, who shine like stars in this generation.* In humanistic culture, a star refers to someone who rose to fame based on their glory. In the kingdom of God, we shine like stars, showing His glory. Philippians 2:15.

God designed and called us to bring the light of hope, wisdom, peace, and healing to those in need. We are the light of the world. Matthew 5:14-16. The credit doesn't go to us but to God. This is the purpose of nobility: to bring service to humanity and honor to the Father. That is what it means to live as Christ, who was the ideal example of this lifestyle.

When I was young, I heard a traveling pastor explain our new identity like this: "You will need the Holy Spirit to translate it into your language." It's like packing the goodness of Heaven into a little carry-on bag. We carry God. The former version of you is gone. Who you are, renewed in Christ, and the potential of what God can do in your soul is beyond dreams. The Bible verse, 2 Corinthians 5:17, teaches that a*nyone who follows Christ becomes brand new, transformed by His love and mercy, a new creation, unlike anything that used to exist.*

You are now a person filled with God's nature. You are the light of the world. The Spirit of God fuels you with wisdom and love. The flame is Christ, and you are the lampstand. When we say yes to God and follow His wisdom, our lives shine like the

sun. That light—the hope of eternal glory and the gift of present peace—is the fire of God, housed in our souls. I'll admit, I'm not sure why I try to paint something of this magnitude with words that feel like crayons. It feels like trying to reproduce Van Gogh with a box of Crayolas. Only God can reveal this to you. Ask Him for revelation and fill up on the Bible. This is a journey of wonder that will never end.

Action Steps

1. **Identify Your "St. Catherine's" Moment:**
   Have you had a moment that brought you to a better place of openness to God, inspired greater love for your family, or even for yourself? Write it down. Reflect on it

2. **Declare Your Identity in Christ:**
   Find verses that speak of your identity. Find verses that talk about being children of God. Reflect on them. Read your favorite aloud each day for a week.

3. **Serve with Nobility:**
   Choose one way to reflect your divine identity in service—through compassion, encouragement, or prayer.
   Write a short note or take a simple action this week that brings God's light to someone else.

The Call to Nobility

For the rest of this chapter, I am going to present ideas that may challenge your current mindset. Before I unpack more of this subject—what it means to be noble and how vital it is that we accept that title—may I make a suggestion? When you come across an idea that offends or feels too grand compared to your current thoughts, pause and pray.

This book is meant to encourage you to listen to God and rely on His wisdom. I hope to inspire you to make it a life practice to bring every thought before God, asking Him to shine His light on it, bringing clarity and courage.

When prolonged pain creates deep grooves—as it does in the brain—it can seem impossible to believe in something new. The idea of confidence and dignity can sound hollow or fake if all you've known is rejection and shame. Nobility can feel foreign and even pretentious.

Our environments shape our self-image over time, forming mental pathways and patterns—what we often call mindsets.

Trauma creates deep riverbeds of negative thinking, shaping our worldview. If you've lived in a cynical pattern for decades, the idea of a renewed life might seem like a childish dream. However, hope remains.

Science now confirms that the brain has an incredible ability to renew and rewire itself—this is called *neuroplasticity*. If you haven't heard of it, I encourage you to research it. I especially recommend Dr. Caroline Leaf's books on the subject. She specializes in helping people recover from brain injuries and severe emotional conditions, using science-based tools and biblical wisdom. Her books, *Who Switched Off My Brain?* And *Cleaning Up Your Mental Mess* was deeply encouraging to me during my concussion recovery. Consider adding her voice to your reading and social media habits—you'll find stories of incredible transformation.

I bring up this science-based point to emphasize what God has said from the beginning: being born again renews us. Neuroplasticity is simply a scientific discovery of what God designed from the start. He created us as pliable, adaptable, and healable beings, capable of growing beyond our past limitations and "glass ceilings." Don't believe that this renewal is only for others—it's for you.

Watch out for those glass ceilings—don't bow to them. Dare to be humble. Agree with God. He knows the darkness you've experienced. The beliefs you've called certainties are no match for His wisdom. God's ways are light and life. No amount of darkness can hold you captive when you turn to Him. And when you feel too weak to move, He will reach into those spaces with tenderness and compassion and lift us. Psalm 3:3.

If the struggle to believe is too heavy, seek help. Surround yourself with people who will speak truth and hope. Faith-centered therapists, experienced pastors, and wise mentors are gifts in the healing process. Your environment matters.

Surround yourself with light—music, media, conversations, and counsel that reflect God's hope. Be vigilant about your influences. If the people or content in your life don't echo God's love and truth, replace them. You are the gatekeeper of your soul.

Accepting the Title

Two words sum up the deepest hunger of the human soul: identity and significance. Throughout history, humanity has asked, *Who am I?* and *Why do I exist?* Without self-awareness, we lack purpose. But the moment we glimpse who we truly are, something shifts inside. We step out of the fog and into the light.

God offers the answers to those questions. He created us—who better to consult? We are children of God, created and redeemed by Christ to live fully and bring healing to others. When we are reborn by His Spirit, our true identity emerges. We are dearly loved children. From that love flows our purpose. Love is creative and redemptive. Whatever we do for a living becomes a calling in the light of God's love.

This new nature includes a renewed mindset. The Holy Spirit becomes our coach, helping us replace old thoughts with God's wisdom. While the transformation in our spirit is immediate, the renewal of our minds takes time. As we shift our focus and agree with God, our inner landscape changes.

Every new mindset we adopt creates physical changes in our brains. Science shows that it takes around two months to form new mental pathways. This is a powerful confirmation of God's design—He wants to reshape us into the glorious beings He intended at the dawn of creation. 2 Corinthians 5:17.

Christ the King saved humanity. Royal blood redeemed us. His blood now heals and flows through you. We do not save ourselves. Only Christ can break the spiritual chains that bind us. Isaiah 61 says, *"The Spirit of the Sovereign Lord is on me, because He has anointed (and qualified) me to preach good news to the poor..."* His grace transforms us, qualifies us, and enables us to live noble lives.

The Bible says that all of this is done to reveal His glory. When we accept Christ, God fills us with His Spirit and invites us to partner in His purposes. We become ambassadors of His love, pointing others to His goodness. The greatest joy in life is seeing someone transformed by love. What a wonder to carry the nature of God.

Why Nobility Matters

Why is it so important to see ourselves as noble?

Because we live up to the labels we believe. As children, we're shaped by the voices around us—parents, teachers, pastors, relatives. If those voices spoke hope and identity, we carry that. If they spoke shame or limitation, we carry that too—until we choose differently.

The good news? We can change the labels. Using the same practices that formed the old mindsets, we can form new paradigms, fueled by God's love. We rebuild our inner world through meditation, reading the Word, worship, and wise relationships.

And one practical word of caution: if peace is your goal, cut back on toxic media. Much of what fills our timelines is filled with anxiety, anger, and cynicism. You are responsible for what shapes your soul.

Nobility is not just a mindset—it's a state of the soul. It belongs to those who choose to embrace it. Daily realignment through humility and truth lifts our lives. God's nature—His glory—fills us with peace, dignity, and hope. John 17:2-5 describes this beautifully.

Just as royal families raise their children with intentionality, God trains us to live as a royal priesthood. When we agree with Him about who we are, we begin to live differently. We shake off sin more easily. We become a source of healing and wisdom to others. This is the noble life.

Foolishness is born of selfishness. But when we follow Christ, our new nature calls us to wisdom. We begin to live with an eternal perspective. We measure our time and tasks carefully. We live with purpose, reflecting the One who redeemed us. Jesus said, *"I do what I see my Father doing."* (John 5:19) This is our guide as well.

And then there's Mary, at the wedding in Cana, offering us one of the most powerful pieces of advice ever spoken: "Whatever He tells you to do, do it." (John 2:5)

Led by the Spirit, there is no limit to what God can do through a willing heart. *"Not by might, not by power, but by My Spirit,"* says the Lord (Zechariah 4:6).

Heaven is calling. You are being invited into a royal role. Not as a figurehead, but as a caregiver of humanity, a priest, a light in the darkness. The Bible says, *"My sheep hear My voice... and they follow Me."* (John 10:27)
He wants to shine through your everyday life.

Action Steps

1. **Rewrite Your Inner Labels**
   Take 10 minutes to list any negative labels you've carried about yourself ("unworthy," "not enough," "failure"). Then write a new list beside it, using biblical truth ("child of God," "redeemed," "qualified," "noble"). Keep the new list somewhere visible and speak it aloud each morning.

2. **Commit to 60 Days of Renewal**

   Choose one daily practice (Scripture reading, prayer, or journaling) and commit to doing it for 60 days. Track your progress and watch for mindset shifts. Neuroplasticity + the Holy Spirit = transformation.

3. **Detox Your Inputs**

   Do a one-week media detox. Remove any music, shows, accounts, or people that cloud your thoughts with anxiety, cynicism, or shame. Fill that time with uplifting content and conversations that echo God's light and truth.

Saints - Old and New

As I sit in this sacred place, St. Catherine's Chapel, I am reminded of her life. Honored for bravery and faith, she led people to a deeper faith, with the wisdom received and written through a miracle of grace. She could not read or write, yet her surrender to God opened her to a miracle. God endowed her with a skill she did not possess naturally: the ability to write.

Saint Catherine is a powerful example of what can happen when we humble ourselves and agree with God. He lifts our lives into the light of His love and grants us significance, anointing our weakness with divine ability. Her divine gift made it possible for her to do what God was calling her to do. Our experiences with gifts will differ, but they will be similar in matters of purpose: to bring peace and to point people to Christ. I encourage you to read the biographies of people throughout history who have followed Christ. Their stories will inspire your surrender.

A brave young believer, St. Catherine, made a bold claim: She could hear the voice of God. This statement was unheard of at that point in history. In our generation, with access to various Bible lexicons and commentaries, we understand her claim as a normal part of life for a believer. The Bible states many times that God answers our prayers. God says, "My sheep hear my voice..." John 10:27. Though modern faith has increased access to understanding the scripture, in her day, it was a radical statement. "I hear God."

Talk about courage! The experience humbled her. Divinely gifted with the ability to write, she documented the precious wisdom gathered during times of prayer and meditation.

This is something profound to pause and reflect on — a lesson we need to ponder. There is little in our culture that resembles this level of humility, commitment, and wonder. We live such distracted, high-speed lives. If we are to become fully alive and noble, claiming the identity and purpose we long for and are called to, something has to change. We have to stop making excuses and make life-altering decisions.

How does that hit you? What are some questions and hungers that arise when you read about a person who committed their life to listening to God, gathering wisdom, and shaping culture by sharing His Word? Is that amazing to you? Do you feel any curiosity about how that could reshape your paradigm and bring you peace?

What would have to change for you to experience something similar? Are you distracted? Do you feel the speed of the wheels spinning beneath and around you? Does the idea of peace feel distant or something that only happens on vacation? One word from God will calm that storm. The whispers are where we find the wisdom.

What needs to change to allow you to hear Him? Expectations? The morning routine? Your willingness to sacrifice time, sleep, or scrolling? Maybe it's an issue of identity: you don't think God would talk to you. Whatever the barrier, pray and ask God to help you take it down. He wants you to know Him. He won't let anything separate you from His love. Romans 8:31. Reciprocate that heart, letting nothing distract you from His love. God wants you to know Him and hear His voice. You are His child.

The Bible gives believers various noble titles: saints, kings, priests, and children of God. These descriptors speak of our redeemed nature. Does this rock your paradigm? Stop a moment and pray, asking God to help you see these labels as He sees them and to help you see yourself within these frames. Make a firm decision to agree with God.

This is not an emotional matter; it is a matter of conviction.

Feelings are trailers. They follow our beliefs. We employ our beliefs to form both excuses and convictions. Rising to wisdom and accepting our noble position is simply a matter of bringing our thoughts into humility and agreeing with God. His thoughts will transform our thinking and beliefs, shaping our convictions and paradigm. The truth is, we are defined by the love and wisdom of God. We are children of God.

As I sit here and watch the sunlight stream through the gold and green-toned stained glass, warming the entire sanctuary with a holy glow, I am reminded of God's whispers to me when I last worshiped here. This glorious temple is a symbol of our life. St. Catherine's, in all her beauty, does not save or heal. It is a temple in which others experience God. This is also true for us. We are merely vessels. We are carriers of the sacred saving grace and messengers of the One who saves.

In the front and center of the cathedral, an almost lifelike statue of Christ on the cross hangs on the stone wall, reminding all of our glorious Savior. The icon inspires us to embrace His example. Dying to self, as the Bible inspires, is not living empty but filled with the Spirit. Christ accomplished everything through the power of the Holy Spirit. Christ did not even raise Himself from the grave, though He had the power to raise others from theirs. The Spirit does the divine work!

We discover the wonder of transformation when we follow Christ, who listened to and followed the Father's wisdom. Jesus lived, died, and was resurrected through the power of the Spirit. This is the lifestyle we are called to emulate. A life for the glory of the Father, but the power of the Spirit — following Christ.

Living nobly is not a performance. It's not a lofty attitude we walk around with. It's not something we produce with good works. We receive nobility the moment we surrender our souls to God. In that sacred moment, there is an invisible exchange of our nature for Christ's. God infuses us with the grace and wisdom of His Spirit. I am agonizing over words to communicate what God gave us as I write this. It is impossible to fully comprehend the immeasurable, incomprehensible gift of the Spirit. We are talking about the same being that participated in the creation of the universe. His power is present to help you and me every day. Inconceivable!

Even if we commit to the daily exploration of the potential of this power, we will never comprehend its capacity or ability, this side of eternity. That's not a stop sign to suggest parking. It's a green light, compelling all of us to a holy challenge of discovery. Proverbs 25:2: "It is the glory of God to conceal a matter; to search out a matter is the glory of kings."

Many years ago, I learned a phrase from a pastor and family therapist, Bob Hamp, who was the first person I heard present the marvel of the connection between spiritual and psychological matters. It made a profound shift in the way I understood life and faith. In his first book, Think Differently, Live Differently, he unpacks the story of our lives in an allegory entitled: The Acrobat. You've got to read this. Through it, I learned that I was living in a cloud of confusion surrounding my identity. The book walks readers through an amazing transformation.

It was Hamp's teaching that first introduced me to this truth: We were never intended to work for love, but from love. We do nothing to earn the title of noble, except agree with God. We are who He says we are. He made, redeemed, and defines us. His love reforms our thinking and inspires all we do. When we live in agreement with His wisdom, the river of His power flows in and through us.

How do we make the shift and accept this nobility? Begin with the first virtue of humility. Make margins of time and pay attention to the disciplines birthed by humility: silence, solitude, and surrender. In those daily margins, ask God to speak to you and teach you the truth. Get into the Bible and search out passages that answer the questions swirling around your soul. God will speak to you. He will give you a picture, impression, or sense of knowing within your imagination. If it lines up with the Bible, you know you're hearing clearly.

In the famous book *Are You My Mother?*, the mother duckling wanders off from her nest before her little one hatches. As he emerges from the nest, he feels the pain of isolation and instinctively goes off to find his mother. He wanders through that first day of life, asking every animal on his path, "Are you my mother?"

The book illustrates our deep longing to find our identity and home. It reveals our two greatest quests: finding ourselves and our people. I like to think of it this way: Discovering ME and where I should BE. I believe this sums up our drive for purpose. We want to live purposefully, but we ache for home.

A purpose based on what we do will never satisfy us without having the *'who'* portion of our needs fulfilled. God has the wisdom to settle these matters. Identity and home are pinnacle searches, both discovered and revealed in the love and wisdom of God. He teaches us the truth of who we are, revealing our identity. Identity is my dwelling. We feel safe and sound within our skin when we agree with God.

Home is our tribe, our community: the collection of dwellings, our people, committed to living in love. We need identity and home.

The Bible is full of messages from God inviting humanity to His heart—home. Jesus speaks to this core need and calls humanity to Himself: "Come to Me." Matthew 11:28. The promise to refresh and heal is deeper than physical strength. This signifies how Christ intended life to be lived, centered on His love. When we find our home in Christ, we find rest, but we also find ourselves. In Him, we live and move and have our being (Acts 17:28).

There is an invisible trap in our first-world, hard-work culture. It's covered with a golden cloud of promise. The shimmer attracts our attention and provokes us to buy in. The lie convinces us to make an idol out of our effort: "If it's meant to be, it's up to me."

Can you relate? I can! My father passed away when I was a child. One result of that tragedy was that my mother needed to work full-time. When a family experiences a death, divorce, or abandonment, the dynamics of roles within the family shift. My mother became a single parent, both mother and father. My brothers and I shifted from children into mini-adults, cooking dinner and cleaning the house—two kids under ten and one teenager. Work ethic? We called it survival.

That life event created three little adults, able to carry life very early. The benefit of that crisis was that we learned we could achieve whatever we wanted if we worked hard enough. That attitude is great for the workforce and bankbook, but not great in soul care and spiritual matters, where surrender is key. Grit cannot give us what grace provides. A hard work ethic has limits in its ability. Self-will is a hurdle to spiritual health. Divine dignity is a gift of grace, not a badge of brawn. A self-willed work ethic reduces the chances of partnering with God.

Self-will blocks our ability to sense spiritual things. God cannot work with individuals who consider themselves wiser than Him. Grit tells us to keep pushing. Humility hands out white flags. A white flag. You know, that thing we interpret to mean we're losing. In the Kingdom of God, the white flag is where winning begins.

We can build quite a kingdom for ourselves with a hard work ethic. But as the Bible says, a rich, self-made person can't enter the Kingdom of Heaven. Matthew 19:23. To enter, they must stop flexing, showing off to confirm their worth.

We live in a world that sells by flexing. Nobility is not defined by accomplishment or accolades. It is defined by the divine DNA within us. We were created by God, in His image, filled with His Spirit, to bring the goodness of Heaven to Earth. "It is He who has made us. We are His people and the sheep of His pasture." Psalm 100:3. We won't discover the truth of who we are and feel at home until we stop flexing and start following Christ.

Love created us. Love is our origin. Love is our home. God is love. Love is the nature of God. This is the reason He told us to make love our greatest aim. He is calling us to make Him the center point of our lives. 1 Corinthians 14:1-4. He's been trying to teach us the way to live from day one. When we listen and go with God, making His love our priority, His wisdom and ways train us for life. Everything lines up. He makes something beautiful out of our lives. No amount of flexing compares to the glory of love and what it accomplishes.

The glory (excellency) of God rests, like a crown of belonging, on the people who follow Him. It's a state of being gifted to us when we lay down our lives to live for Christ. This surrender lifts us into nobility. Make no mistake; just as Jesus prayed for help to endure the cross, we need the grace of God to help us lay down our lives. Dying to self is not a glamorous, dramatic event. It is a private, sometimes painful, journey of complete surrender. And it's only possible through His Spirit. The Spirit leads us into surrender and sustains us, just as He did for Christ in the wilderness. We turn away from ourselves and into the divine plan for our lives, and the adventure begins. We will spend a lifetime and into eternity discovering the fullness of this adventure. I have not expressed the full scope of His heart because I can't fathom or define it. But I've done my best.

Wonderland

Yes, I'm still sitting in St. Catherine's. It's taken hours in this little rock haven to listen, ponder, and write to you. As I do, I'm reflecting on the wonder of God and the thought that He has made us in His image. I would love to sit in this rocky wonderland and worship Him for the rest of my life, but my work is beyond these walls. As I leave, I will kneel and praise and pray, giving thanks to God, praying for you, anticipating what He will do in your life. You are His: redeemed, righteous, and noble.

"Oh, what manner of love the Father has given to us — that we would be called children of God." 1 John 3:1. This is how He loves us! He has made us His own. Noble.

Perhaps the most important reason we press into this revelation of being noble is because of the deep longing in our hearts to find a home. God's redemption transforms us into vessels of honor the moment we believe. Our chains fall away, and we find the divine embrace we long for. We surrender ourselves most fully to the love of God when we consider ourselves worthy of this sonship. He has made us worthy. We enjoy the fullness of belonging when we believe. If it feels like an impossible dream, don't be discouraged. Keep leaning into this wonder. He will change your mind as you daily fill your soul with His truth.

We can nestle deep into the role of sonship and thrive in that place. A lack of nobility causes us to resist His love. That doesn't deter Him. God is an endearing Father who waits for our return. Seeing the truth and turning to Him restores us to childlike joy and peace! No greater joy exceeds the wonder of being known and loved. It is the longing of our lives.

God reveals the truth: you are loved and worthy. Restored to a relationship with God, you are a child of the King. You are noble. God's love has a constant flow of life and wisdom springing out into our hearts. Inspiration flows and feeds our identity, reminding us of the truth.

As I write, wrapped in the wonder of St. Catherine's, I consider the legacy of this woman who lived with a passion for Christ. She radically affected her generation and inspired generations to come to consider what God will do to guide His people.

Her life continues to inspire humanity to listen to God. What a noble dream! This happens when we surrender our lives. God lifts us so we can lift others.

Discovering this wonder is your destiny and mine. We are becoming more fully alive, day by day, as we learn the truth and implement it in our lives. God has redeemed us to live aware of His presence and full of His light—every day! "Days of Heaven here on Earth". Deuteronomy 11:2. This becomes our reality when we live in that awareness of God.

I like how Bob Hamp, mentioned earlier in the chapter, describes this in the book *Think Differently, Live Differently*: "It is always and only about becoming ourselves within our circumstances."

This process happens right in the middle of our story.

Pivotal Prayer Moments

Through Bob's teachings and that powerful book, I began to pray differently—bringing my deepest wrestlings and wounds to God. I learned to release the pain and how to receive wisdom from God. It was a prayer experience I had not known before reading the book.

It's a powerful thing to discover that God not only hears—He answers. Again, the humility step comes into play. I humbled myself, prayed, and believed that God would speak, just as He said He would. John 10:27 says, "My sheep hear my voice…"

Through that new life skill, my inner world made a powerful pivot. I prayed and received life-altering insight in return. This became my new processor for pain, grief, anxiety, problems, and fear. One word from God changes everything.

These are the two simple but profound prayers I learned to practice from Hamp's teaching. They have been game changers, especially when my soul feels unsteady and my confidence has slipped away. Use them in your prayer time today and throughout the week, and be prepared to journal what you discover in the silence after the prayers. Make time to listen, wait, and rest in god's goodness as you pray them.

"Father, tell me the truth about You."

Journal the words of hope and wisdom discovered not only in prayer but as you go about your day. If there is one thing I've learned about God, it is that He speaks to those who cherish His inspiration.

"Father, tell me the truth about me."

Journal what you receive. God's thoughts are always in line with His Word. You can expect words filled with grace and hope. He always leads with kindness. Give thanks and agree with God.

You may choose to make these a daily practice this week for your action steps. Keep a pen handy! God will answer. He always leads us with kindness and heals us with light. Don't allow any message of fear to have the mic during these times of prayer. Focus on God's unfailing love for you—and listen.

Actions Steps

1. **Continue to Create Sacred Space in Your Day:** Make time each day for silence, solitude, and surrender. In those quiet moments, ask God to speak to you. Read Scripture, journal, and listen. Prioritize presence over productivity.

2. **Reframe Your Identity with God's Word:**

    Find Bible passages that affirm your identity as a child of God (e.g., 1 Peter 2:9, Romans 8:17). Write them down. Speak them aloud daily. Let them replace false labels and reshape your self-view.

3. **Practice Grace over Grit:** Let go of self-reliance. In areas where you tend to strive, stop and pray instead. Striving creates anxiety and tension. Grace is power without pressure. Ask God to show you where surrender—not effort—is the path forward. Allow His Spirit to lead your daily work, relationships, and decisions.

Faithful

Years ago, I sat with a broken woman, angered by the divorce of her parents and hardened by the selfishness of men who had used her. A powerful conversation unfolded. She was pregnant and at a crossroads moment of decision. I asked about her boyfriend and whether they had planned on a future together, marriage perhaps? Her answer was stone cold: "Marriage? Does anyone believe in that fairytale anymore?"

Her hopelessness was heartbreaking and palpable. For a moment, it was hard to breathe. The pain had created dark definitions of marriage and the potential of love. I wanted to provide an answer while also tending to her broken heart. I took a moment for a silent prayer, allowing me to calibrate to wisdom before I answered her.

"Fairytale? Is that what you consider it? Isn't marriage love with loyalty? Doesn't everyone want love with loyalty? Just because others have failed at it doesn't mean we should stop believing and working for that kind of love."

Her expression changed. I had uncovered something she believed in, or at least longed for — loyalty. With the altered definition, and perhaps because of empathy, she agreed. Loyalty rooted in love is the greatest experience in life. Marriage, as God designed and presents it in the Bible, is the sacred oath of loyalty between a man and a woman.

Having been through the war zone for years in my marriage, feeling alone and resentful for years, I understood her perspective. I remembered the sting of neglect and the painful assumptions and definitions created in its wake. The fairytale perspective of love portrayed in the film industry doesn't show the reality of life or the relational skills required in building a marriage.

Character is the inner strength that empowers us to love with loyalty. Even the magic within my four words is not a scene from a movie, but a lifestyle of praying, learning, and reforming mindsets, attitudes, and actions. Those elements of character can create sparks to nurture love. The fire of loyalty is stoked in the sacred place we build into our lives. When we set our faces like flint, focused on the wisdom of God, we discover the magic within His wisdom and love. Setting our face like flint is an ancient term referring to the sharpening of a stone, turning it into a weapon. When we make the decision that leads to transformation, we are like that stone. God honors our humility and provides all we need for change. His nature reforms ours. His nature becomes ours.

If we choose to believe in love and wisdom, it will transform our cynicism into hope. I've heard miracle stories of people changing overnight. For most of us, it will take time. This was the case for my husband and me. The change was slow. It would take years of commitment to the building process. We made that decision, and it was worth it! The magic of these divine virtues, with the love of God inspiring us, created something pretty wonderful. And we are still growing strong!

That is why I share our story, woven throughout the book. I was convinced we were on a crash course to ruin. Yet, wisdom changed everything. The magic, of course, is the power of God's love and how it can build something beautiful. Every broken story is another opportunity for God's redeeming love to show up and amaze those within that story. All ashes have the potential to be reformed into beauty.

Humble, Grateful, Noble, Faithful. That mural will stay with us for as long as we both live, testifying to the power of wisdom. It has served as a constant reminder concerning this life and our walk of faith.

One word is stacked on the other, reminding us of the process of change and the time required for growth. When we step into humility, there's no telling the doors that will fling open and the wisdom that will follow. We know this as we go the distance on the path of humility, open to the virtues. It leads us forward and makes us faithful!

All of us need visual inspiration to keep us diligent in the fight. I'm not talking physically, though that's helpful. I'm talking about the ability to see hope for our future. If we hold up wisdom and virtue like lampposts in our lives, they will continue to speak, offering the answers we desperately need. These words that we search out and gather as guideposts for our lives remind us that God gives wisdom to build the beautiful matters of love and life. We just have to listen, write them down, and walk by them.

Like keys from heaven, those words unlocked the strength I needed for life. Each step in humility, each moment preferring gratitude over greed, one choice after another, learning what it meant to be noble, instead of prideful, provided new insight and understanding.

Every choice to practice gratitude led to a new outcome of happiness. Gratitude radically improves the ability to see hope in the future.

It allows us to see our entire life differently. When we see the past differently, counting our blessings, we can see the future differently.

Gratitude washes over us and changes our perspective on the past, present, and future. When I started practicing gratitude, the fresh perspective gave me eyes to see what had happened between my former collection of negative memories. I started a new history book in my soul, one that recorded a better story of my life. God had kept His Word, rescued me a thousand times. With a healed vision of my past, I could see hope for the future. God will always open doors in my life. What is there to fear?

Before I could rise to any level of strength in the matter of faithfulness, I had to conquer the mountain that shadowed it. The hardest magic word for me to accept was the identity-shaping perspective of being noble. I had a tough time seeing myself as noble. The root issue came from the deep-seated idea that people were the ones who decided my value. I counted the votes throughout my life, and the results created a blaring message: I was not worthy of the word. Do your opinion polls sound the same? Many people share this experience. Again, these feelings did not reflect the entire truth of my history, but a select group of negative memories I had collected to that point in life.

Self-esteem is formed through words and experiences in childhood. We collect and sort those experiences and store them in our souls. Somehow, it's easier to believe the negative narratives picked up on the path. Those lies that teach that physical appearance, achievements, intellect, and wealth measure our value rise like billboards.

Society operates by measuring, comparing, and then approving or rejecting. It's a painful, punishing cultural norm. These mirage standards are impossible to achieve and leave the soul feeling unworthy, unwanted, or worse, celebrated for shallow reasons that soon evaporate, creating a sense of insecurity.

This is the reason that developing a spiritual practice of gathering definitions from God, through reading the Bible, meditating on it, and praying, is so powerful! The discipline privately acknowledges the power of words and the choice to make God's opinion and wisdom our north star. His Word redeems our definitions and reforms our paradigms as we exchange our old labels for His definitions of grace and dignity.

God says we are noble. His Word is truth and is the plumb line for our lives. He raises the bar—and lifts us to it. We merely

agree. Nobility has nothing to do with human standards. Only a revelation from God, shifting our minds from this plastic culture to His divine dignity, can create this deep confidence, contentment, and peace. A divinely inspired definition solidifies our sense of being. Realizing that we are reborn, holy children of God, accepting ourselves as noble, is essential to the strength required for faithfulness.

Faithfulness is only as strong as our core beliefs. If there is no sense of nobility, the fortitude of our faithfulness will tremble with every circumstance and emotion. When we accept God's grace and see ourselves differently, our responses also change. This revelation of God's love plants and roots us with a core level of security. Those who are secure do not waver. They are faithful.

Do you see it? Faithfulness is not about your performance. People can fake that veneer. True faithfulness is core-level love. God alone can produce that in us. The fruit of the Spirit is love.

Developing Strength

How do we develop that strength? As I mentioned, it begins with acknowledging our world and our current condition. We are swimming in an ocean of humanism and often believe it to be reality. Our world is hard-set on cynicism. We define people by their failures for a lifetime, yet give them fifteen minutes of fame for their strength. We remember losses and forget wins. Once people fail, that's it! No mercy! They remain in that dungeon forever. This is the cynical cycle of our culture and was the way I saw myself—and others.

By age twenty, I felt imprisoned by the many crimes of my youth. I felt hopeless. Oh, religion offered me a side hustle to earn comfort, but it never paid in full. Through the lens of religion, nobility looked like a pyramid scheme, and I could never sell enough to fit in. Religion does that to us. It's based on the human endeavor to please God. The Gospel is the total opposite. I knew that theoretically, but not literally. I was stuck in the hustle.

"While we were still sinners, Christ died for us." Romans 5:8 He swept in, paid the ransom, and pulled us off the highway to hell. In a flash, He exchanged our rags and ashes for glory and goodness—making us holy.

Here's the challenging part—the mind-bender. The moment we pivot and walk with Christ, our spirit is completely holy. I know! Who can explain that one? Unfortunately, our minds, wills, and emotions don't change at the same rate. The soul enters a process called sanctification. It's the slow-motion version of what happens in our spirit when we are born again. But God fulfills His promise. He takes us from ashes into a state of wonder—beauty. Isaiah 61:3.

Humility, gratitude, and nobility are the virtues that align us with God's purpose for our lives. They move us into a noble mindset and strengthen our stance, allowing us to endure the storms of life. These virtues strengthen and steady us. When we lose sight of hope in long seasons of drought, or what St. John of the Cross called the "dark night of the soul", we can draw comfort from the deep well created by these divine gifts. That deep well refreshes our souls and reminds us that our source will never run dry.

Action Steps

1. **Practice Daily Humility and Prayer:** Begin each day with a humble heart, asking God for wisdom and strength. Prayer aligns our will with God's and opens us to transformation.

2. **Cultivate Gratitude:** Regularly count and record your blessings. Shift your focus from what is lacking or painful to what is good and hopeful. Gratitude rewires our perspective toward faithfulness.

3. **Embrace Your Noble Identity in Christ:** Meditate on God's Word that affirms your worth and nobility as His child. Reject societal lies about worth and anchor your identity in God's truth, strengthening your core belief and fortitude.

The Nature of Faith

As I write this chapter on faithfulness, I am streamside, along the Fraser River, a tributary just outside Granby, Colorado. My husband is an avid fly fisherman, and I am an outdoors girl through and through. Nature captivates me. Whether it's mountains, forests, rivers, oceans, or otherwise, just get me outside.

As I overlook the rocky-lined river and listen to the water dancing along, I can't help but think of what it leads to: the mighty Colorado. Hundreds of miles downstream, this sparkling ribbon that hypnotizes my soul will become a thunderous roar, overwhelming all other sounds of nature.

This is what faith is like. It begins as a sweet stream. Tiny drops of understanding concerning God's love and wisdom, like the melting snow on the mountains, trickle into our souls. Like the warm western sun turning frozen crystals into droplets of water, the perfect, pure thoughts of God melt our fears and broken paradigms. It washes over our thinking—purifying our perspective. Fresh streams of hope and peace carve new pathways within us. He makes all things beautiful—including us. Ecclesiastes 3:11.

Move with me from the mountain view to some scientific facts: Science calls those streams neuropathways—riverbeds within our minds. These patterns set our minds to respond to the matters of life. Our minds become set in the rhythms we accept as normal. They are matters of mindset.

As I mentioned earlier, we can reform these riverbeds of thinking. Science confirms what God has said forever: We are transformed by the renewing of our minds. Romans 12:2. His Word can replace old thoughts and create a magnificent river of life.

The sky is the limit when it comes to the renewal of our minds. According to the Bible, we can think like Christ. Shocking! But it's in there—1 Corinthians 2:16. Wisdom and love flow constantly from God toward humanity. The divine gift resets our brains to function with patterns of courage and confidence. Spiritual renewal reforms the soul, our mind, will, and emotions. The Bible refers to it as the fruit or outcome of a life led by the Holy Spirit. Galatians 5:22-23.

A tiny stream of belief can rise and reform our existence.

When we feed that stream, it can become a flood of truth, eroding walls of anger, renovating the landscape of our lives. Goodness will overcome evil. Romans 12:21. It's a mighty force of faith. Like the wonderful waters of the Colorado, we can harness the energy of truth to benefit our lives.

If you feel like faith is gone, or if you're hungry for more, if you feel weak and struggle with faithfulness, remind yourself that you are not alone. God will meet you where you are. He will carry you and give you strength. It begins with a divine seed planted in us when we hear the hope found in the Bible.

That's where my story took a giant pivot. I had come to the end of myself and was ready for change. On a normal day in my laundry room, you could say I came clean with God. Because I had more interaction with doctrines, religious requirements, and public opinion than a private lifestyle of listening to and walking with God, there was a lot to clean up. My addiction to the opinions of others had made a mess of my soul. It paralyzed me.

When we live by the opinions of others, we never learn to think for ourselves. We are governed by the thoughts of others. Our mind is the drafting table of life. God wants to meet us there and teach all things regarding life and godliness.

A mind enslaved to following people will never discover this potential. That was my problem. My heart was longing for a God-size dream, but my mind couldn't rise above public opinion.

Finally, I admitted to myself that I was not who I wanted to be. A mushroom cloud of anger was brewing within. Doubts about God, anger about the state of the church, and with myself for being okay with it for so long, had formed an internal storm I could no longer ignore. I felt disillusioned about life, rejected by people, and far from God.

For decades, fear blinded me, and I couldn't see life, God, or myself accurately. There was a deep, undeniable hunger to know the truth and find peace. The hunger could not be ignored or pacified any longer. I had to know the truth and find freedom. In that little laundry room, I admitted my doubts and whispered a simple prayer.

If you are real, I need you to show me.

It was a simple prayer. Simplicity is often the most powerful pathway to change. That prayer opened the door to a life-changing transformation of faith and hope. Here's the thing about raw honesty: it opens and positions us to learn.

Pain is an articulate teacher. It somehow softens our souls and opens our ears. If we resist bitterness, pain will point to the better way. In that space, the Holy Spirit invites us onto the narrow road leading upward. Humility is the gateway to that path. In the laundry room, I resisted bitterness and chose humility.

There was a hard pivot that day. The laundry wasn't the only thing that came clean. I changed at a core level, and everyone benefited, beginning at home. There was an instant light that ignited within, but it took time to learn how to shine consistently and to surrender each façade and failing tactic.

A Cinderella Story

In the opening chapter, I used the example of magic words to describe how these virtues open doors to reformation. Our childish understanding of magic creates unrealistic expectations of change. We hope it to be a 'poof' experience, but the wonder of transformation requires much more time. These magic words changed my life, but there was no 'bippity-boppity-boo' about them.

Character develops slowly. For the sake of my family, I wish it were only a day! I wish I had known then what I know now.

I wish I had been who I am today for my kids decades ago. But this is life. We live and we learn. I have no regrets, and trust me, it's taken decades of shedding those shame patterns. I was stuck in sorrow for so long. The sorrow had painted my entire existence black. Grace called me out. Every step closer to God creates an unshakable soul. He led me through choices that washed my perspective. That clean new perspective allowed me to see the past with greater clarity. God had been present and active in my life all along.

There is a human tendency in all of us to see one successful path as a formula or recipe. Refuse the recipes of others. God wants to reveal His love and wisdom to you, personally, privately. Decide for yourself to pay the price and make the sacrifice of forming a lifestyle of solitude, silence, and prayer - both to know and worship God and discover the treasure of wisdom He has in store for you. The Bible and the Spirit are all you need for this sacred discipline.

Be ready for wonder. A life anchored in the secret place always leads to adventure. Prime example: the life of Mary. I love the example of this woman of faith, who has two famous lines in the Scriptures:

Let everything God said be true in my life. Luke 1:38.

Whatever He says, do it. John 2:5.

What an example! And what a gift to make statements of faith of that caliber. Doesn't that stir a fire in you to live bravely and learn what God wants for your life? He created you for a purpose! First, for love: to know His love for you and bring that love to humanity. Second, use your skills to help others. Living an exceptional life is about these core matters: love and wisdom.

Re-read those inspirations from Mary. Feel the divine invitation within them. Live like Mary, and your life will be full! Known for her great commitment to a virtuous life, she exemplifies a life guided by God's Word. Total surrender and amazing outcomes. Get all in with Jesus.

From Cinders to Saints

One of my life's passions is mentoring. I encourage you to pray for and find a mentor. This will help you with that all-in lifestyle. Here are a couple of pointers for finding a mentor. With this encouragement, let me provide this helpful truth: There are 'five-minute mentors' who make a one-time deposit into your life. There are also five-year mentors, who walk with you for a season. Pursue both. There are very few lifetime mentors, as the Holy Spirit is our true lifetime mentor.

As you look for these champions of faith, find someone older with years of wisdom to offer. Think of them as fine wine; the older, the better. Friends offer encouragement and some knowledge; mentors provide time-tested wisdom. This addition will help you stay true to the quest and press through hard seasons. While searching for that person or people, develop instant mentors by reading biographies of people of faith. These were the first mentors of my life: Mother Teresa, Sojourner Truth, Martin Luther, Billy Graham, Oral Roberts, Amy Carmichael, and countless others I met only in the pages of their biographies. There is so much to glean from the lives of brave, wise people.

Something powerful happens when we make the pursuit of wisdom the principal thing. That commitment to growth magnetizes you. It will attract great mentors. A good mentor will guide and encourage you in the steps of faith, pointing you to personal spiritual reliance on the Bible and a lifestyle of listening to the Holy Spirit. I cannot overemphasize the second detail. Great mentors are not looking for followers; they are eager to see your reliance on God increased, making you unshakeable in faith.

This journey of growth begins with moments alone with God. In the ashes of our lives, the cinders, we can recognize that pride will not produce what we long for. We want success in various forms, but that doesn't produce peace. Peace is a spiritual matter. It's a matter of the heart. From cinders to royalty isn't just for fairytales. God takes the ashes of our lives and transforms us into someone beautiful. This is what the heart demands, and it will not be denied. Peace is the oxygen of the soul. No peace means no life—no matter what you own. No amount of worldly success can create peace and satisfy the soul.

My Cinderella moment happened in the laundry room with my prayer: *If you're real, I need You to show me.*

What is your authentic prayer? Have you located yourself? Acknowledge where you are and your spiritual need. God is waiting to turn your ashes into something beautiful.

Obstacles of Faith

At the point when I voiced that pivotal prayer, I had already experienced enough of God's goodness to be convinced of His love for me, but something was disrupting the flow of faith. Something was undermining those God encounters: It was that broken paradigm that kept telling me I was only loved IF I performed. Some people call it a religious spirit.

Oddly, religion is the biggest obstacle between God and people. Religion is man's attempt to connect with God. It turns people into puppets. Religion will reduce God into a cruel taskmaster and veiled judge, and people into mere pawns for someone's vision. It is a pride-based approach, hindering divine connection and conversation. Religious ideologies derail people. It distracts, misinforms, and separates us from an honest, open connection with God.

This is not a modern issue. The problem originated in the Garden of Eden. The serpent convinced Eve of his better path to divinity. She was already full of God's nature and walked with Him daily. Nevertheless, the devil deceived her into believing she was missing something and needed more.

The Pharisees continued with that religious mindset for generations. They added hundreds of laws and requirements for believers to practice. Christ pointed to the Pharisees, making them the living illustration of his sermons on this evil tendency.

It's just as true today. Be sober about this matter. God saves us through grace. Cultivate and guard your faith in the saving grace of God. As we look into that grace, He gifts us with faith. Faith functions like glasses, lenses through which we see and believe. By grace, through faith, God opens our eyes to our need for a spiritual awakening. We see with the heart, and if we agree with God, our spirit comes to life. God's gift of faith endows us with sight and life. We can honestly say, "Once I was blind, but now I see."

When you're tempted to fall for that human nature, comparison-minded, "work for it" default, remind yourself: The spiritual life modeled by Christ is not a scorecard of performance, as the Pharisees suggested. It's the life force of God, pure love and wisdom, made possible through Christ and experienced in us by the power of the Holy Spirit. Grace inspires every step, allowing us to walk in this amazing faith.

Action Steps

1. **Daily Renew Your Mind**: Set aside time each day to read Scripture and meditate on God's promises.

2. **Replace old, fear-based thoughts with God's truth.** Even 5-10 minutes consistently can carve new neuropathways of hope and courage.

3. **Pray with Honesty and Humility**: You can be honest with God. If you're struggling with doubt, work it out with Him. *"If you are real, show me."* Faith grows through humility and openness. Allow God time to shape you, and trust the slow but sure transformation.

Growing Faith

Faithfulness—that full measure of faith shaping our character—grows when we live from God's love. There is merit in being connected to a good church. There is a significant benefit in gleaning wisdom from a mentor. Neither of these elements, however, can replace private worship, prayer, and study. Our personal daily journey with God is the root system of our strength.

God intended for us to link arms with other thriving people in a community of faith, which we call the church. The added help of a mentor fuels even more strength in our development. The Bible describes a healthy church as a group of people who invite a corporate approach to spiritual investments. That means many people are filling up on the Bible's wisdom and sharing love with each other. A healthy church displays other attributes, beginning with acts of charity to care for widows, orphans, and those who are sick and impoverished. Good worship in music and the teaching of the Bible inspire people to greater love and faith.

Acts of mercy for those in the community knit hearts together and show the nature of God to the world. These are some attributes to help you consider where you belong.

Find community in a place that promotes God's wisdom for life, identity, love, marriage, and family. These are the foundation stones of wellness. We must build our lives on His Word if we intend to follow Christ. Find a church that focuses on God's Word for guidance and encouragement. That's how faith grows. Jeremiah says it so well: Your words were found, and I ate them, and they were the joy and the rejoicing of my heart. Jeremiah 15:16

Remember, the most significant growth comes from daily disciplines, not weekly church visits. For physical health, you would never eat all your meals on Sunday and starve yourself on the weekdays. You would never consider a lifestyle of eating once a week, thinking that you would rather sleep in than eat. You would be a mess living like that, or worse, die from starvation. Right? You eat food daily. And when you want to feel strong and healthy, you choose what you eat, realizing that food is fuel. Right?

Think of this analogy as you develop your spiritual health. Treat your spirit like a nutritional bank to resource your life.

Plan a healthy diet of daily food and wine, in spiritual terms, and add layers of mentoring and time with other Jesus-followers to build that healthy soul.

Battlefield Faith

It is important to state that as you make this pursuit for inner health and build your life from the inside out, you will experience days, even seasons, that feel like a battlefield. There will be days when your body feels off and your mind is overwhelmed with life's stress and distractions. The war is on! That doesn't mean faith doesn't work or God doesn't speak. The Bible says, The battle belongs to the Lord, 2 Chronicles 20:15. That doesn't mean you don't fight. You simply don't fight like you would on your own.

Wisdom wins wars. Ask God for wisdom concerning the specifics in life. Be ready to gather the gifts of wisdom that start coming your way. The battle in moments like these is over the wellness and peace within your heart. We fight this fight with light. Surround yourself with promises from God, positivity from your anchor beliefs, and good friends who will echo these messages.

The battle was won long before we realized we were in a war. Jesus already defeated the devil. The light crushed the darkness. All we do at this point is stand and claim the prize.

We overcome evil with good. As we worship God, we see the truth. He is greater. Being His child means being endowed with strength. He suits us up in His armor, the armor of God. We don't suit up to sit on the sidelines. Turn away from fear. Turn your full attention to Jesus. He leads us to victory. Learn the function of these pieces of armor in Ephesians 6:11-18. God is with you. Ask God: What do I need to know right now?

Ask God for wisdom for the war. Don't fight alone. Use these mentors for added wisdom and encouragement. Fight the good fight! Don't listen to fear! The enemy wants to reduce you to a slave of fear with his slideshow of doom. Turn away from that distraction and keep your eyes on Jesus, the Commander-in-Chief. He leads you in triumph and victory. 2 Corinthians 2:14. Keep the Bible as your source for each battle. You will triumph over your enemies.

The word of God is infinitely stronger than the threats of darkness. God's Word is pure power, filling our minds with truth, wisdom, peace, and joy.

Fear is an ancient enemy. David said it this way, "Even when I walk through the valley of the shadow of death, I will fear no evil. You are with me. Your rod and your staff comfort me." Psalm 23:4. Turn your attention to God and worship Him. He has given us His armor and teaches us how to win, with wisdom from above.

Not every struggle is spiritually based. Sometimes we make health choices that affect our wellness. The issue may be a natural element related to the care of your body. You may be in need of sleep, better nutrition, more exercise, or water. The spirit is willing, but the body is weak. It happens to all of us.

When we neglect our physical health, our mental and spiritual health are affected. Know yourself. Care for your body. When our bodies are shouting, we can't hear anything else. One of my dearest mentors, Betty Southard, a speaker and author from Southern California, taught me that sometimes the most spiritual thing you can do is take a nap.

Core-level Faith

The Word has a self-fulfilling power. Give it time, and it will prove itself. Isaiah 61:11 Initial insecurity is normal. That's your mind trying to rationalize God's wisdom. Give it time. Time and experience will prove that God's wisdom is the source of all life and hope. Don't react to fears with more fear; this only feeds them. Instead, starve fear by giving your attention to thoughts about faith. Feed your faith. Pursue wisdom in the Word, through podcasts, reading, or sermons at church. These are moments for you to take in the Word and let it nourish you, turning your sorrow into joy, drowning out the voice of fear.

The light of God's wisdom directs us toward the best options and choices. Remind yourself that it's His thoughts that lead to peace. His Word tells us the truth. Shame has a voice of its own. It tells us that a life of wisdom and peace is for someone else. Wisdom tells us otherwise. It convicts us and compels us to shake off selfishness and resist the tendency to wallow in guilt and shame. Redemption is a gift, not something earned. Shame will always tell you there's a bill to pay. Wrong! Jesus paid it all. You have a direct path to the wisdom of God. His wisdom is a gift to all.

Remember the humility chapter: agree with God. That means denying the feelings of lust, shame, guilt, whatever is contrary to the Word of God. What He says is true.

Humility agrees with God. Faith takes root in that place. God's love will prove His word is true. Keep fighting for that seed. Resist every thought that tells you that you don't deserve it. The noble stance of dignity reminds you—you were born again. Your feelings are not the prophet of your life unless you surrender to them. Don't! It's that simple. Faith starts as a stream. God is the source. Center your focus on the positive words of hope from God. Live from that source, and the stream will grow into a river. Stand in that river until it rises and washes over your life. If you stand still, you will see, God is faithful and true. Exodus 14:13.

Faith Lifts Us

Faith can look like a mirage to those who are struggling. If that's you, take heart. Psalm 34:18 reads, God is close to the brokenhearted and saves those crushed in spirit. If that's what you need, read it again. God wants you to know He is not asking you to do anything beyond your strength. The weakness that paralyzes you can work in your favor. Faith is a gift.

We can cultivate faith by listening to the Spirit, reading the Bible, praying, meditating, and worshiping God. Faith starts out small, in a seed form for everyone. Our weakness becomes the conduit for God's strength and goodness. He honors faith as small as a mustard seed and meets it with grace, moving mountains. Our weakness allows us to see the preferred connection and ideal flow of faith.

A wide-open heart is all that's needed. A humble heart, filled and flooded with God Himself, is a gateway to great things. Weakness gets us to a state of strength faster than a strong will. It's all about openness and humility. You may thank God in the end for this temporary condition. Temporary, because God always turns ashes into beauty and weakness into strength.

Without faith, it is impossible to please God. Hebrews 11:6 Years ago, hearing that verse made me feel like I would never be a strong Christian. That's for those super-Christians. After decades of walking with God, I have realized who He is and His nature. Listen to this descriptor of Him: He will let nothing separate us from His love. Romans 8:31 Since that's true, how can my lack of faith separate me from Him? It goes back again to the topic of humility. Openness.

What does God say? He gives grace to the humble. James 4:6 Grace makes the impossible possible. He gives faith to those who need it. Ask and keep on asking. Faith will rise when we look to God.

Think of the joy you feel when your loved one opens a special gift you chose for them. Think of the happiness in your heart. That is what God feels when we accept His gift. When we accept the gift of God through Jesus Christ, His joy is complete, and our joy is just getting started. When faith seems small, ask God to increase your faith. He will happily answer that prayer!

Dealing with issues of religious prejudice, bad experiences, doubts, etc., and being real with God is the birthplace of growth. Each matter needs to be met with mercy. Have mercy on every person who was a hindrance to your faith. Recognize they are wrestling just like you and may have hidden battles of fear or pride. Have mercy on them. Let God sort that out. Shake it off and move toward the light of God.

Take the same stand regarding your weaknesses. Recognize and repent of the choices you made in fear or pride. Mercy has an amazing ability to help us shake off old thinking and step into agreement with God. When you feel weak in faith, don't be afraid! God is compassionate in our weaknesses. Be honest and ask Him to comfort you and increase your faith.

The Seed of Faith

Faith requires agreement. The humble process of hearing God's wisdom and agreeing with it creates faith. It's a constantly increasing, rising tide of hope that becomes faith. That's what happens when we listen to God and agree. Not only do we gain confidence in His Word, nature, and promises, but we also gain confidence for the future. We walk boldly because we know God is our Father. He is our Shepherd to lead, guide, and provide. If we waver through ignorance or weakness, He will guide and lead us on the best path.

Take a moment and thank God for how far He has already led you! He who started the good work in you is still at work! Philippians 1:6 Ponder and let gratitude add to your hope. It is a powerful daily discipline.

Maybe you're not ready to throw a praise party. Maybe you're questioning your beliefs? That's okay. God understands our wrestling. Christ's disciples said the same thing. They wrestled to believe.

Are you saying, "I believe, but my faith is small?" No worries, Jesus said that if our faith was micro-sized, we could transform the landscape of our lives. Matthew 17:20.

Don't be afraid to only have a fragment of faith. Bring it to God. He only wants your openness. He's not looking for an expert but a willing heart. Find the small seed you can believe in and start there. Agree with God and move forward. Even a little faith is powerful enough to move mountains.

Another reader is saying, I've been doing this a long time, and I live solidly in my faith. Dear friend, I would encourage you not to settle here! Keep asking! Keep seeking! Keep knocking! Matthew 7:7 There is MORE! God is ready to open additional doors of strength, wisdom, compassion, and everything required to make you strong and courageous, like Jesus. Years ago, I created a personal motto. May this also inspire you: "Never settle for being an expert when you could live as an explorer."

Before we move into the action steps for the future, I invite you to pray this prayer:

Father,

I commit to live humbly and look to You. Thank you for meeting me where I am. Thank you for the amazing grace that removed all guilt, shame, fear, selfishness, and pride. Thank you for saving me through Christ.

I agree with You. You said I am your child and I'm dearly loved. It boggles my mind, but I agree with Your Word that says You have made me holy. Hebrews 10:10

Teach me what that means and help me shake off every thought that contradicts this truth.
I commit myself to learning what it means to be noble and to living as Your child. Thank you for loving and saving me. I ask that You give me an understanding of Your wisdom. I want to agree with You but need Your help to do it. Increase my faith. Enlarge my capacity to believe and walk with You. Thank you, Lord.

Amen - let it be.

Action Steps

1. **Continue each Day with Scripture and Prayer:**
   If you're not sure where to start in your Bible reading, try the book of John, Proverbs, or Psalms. Read a Bible passage and pray, meditate on God's goodness or wisdom revealed within the passage. Let God's Word nourish your spirit first thing, anchoring your heart in truth and hope.

2. **Journal your story of faith:**
   Write down insights from your daily readings, prayers, and moments of gratitude. Recording your faith journey helps you notice growth and reminds you of God's faithfulness on tough days.

3. **Connect Weekly with a Faith Mentor or Group of believers who are committed to following Christ:**
   Commit to regular meetings with a mentor or small group, those who prioritize the Bible and protect matters of faith. These relationships encourage and keep your faith strong.

From Ashes to Beauty

I humbly recognize that your story is not my story. Though we share common battles, fears, and experiences, we are not the same. Our paradigms and attitudes, our skills and strengths have been informed and formed by our environments. My battles may not be yours. Your fears may be completely different from those that plague my soul. What is the same is our source of hope and peace. Don't let the difference in our stories distract you from the universal power of these virtues. These stones of strength and wisdom that shaped my life are powerful in every life. The greatest of them all is that key virtue of humility. All wisdom and understanding begin with humility.

All the work behind this book was invested for this reason: Wisdom builds life and provides energy to sustain it. The greatest thing I can do in life is encourage people to look to Christ, the author and finisher of our faith. Hebrews 12:2. All wisdom comes from God the Father, and Christ came to pave the way for us. John 14:6 says no one comes to God the Father without first coming to Christ. He is the Way. John 14:16

The wisdom needed to restore what has been stolen or broken in your story is available. When we pursue wisdom through genuine humility, we start moving in the right direction. We open our souls to the wisdom that will heal and help us. With wisdom as the principal thing and humility leading our endeavor, the sky is the limit.

All virtues are encapsulated with titles—words like mercy, grace, forgiveness, love, and dozens of others. For me, the words that lifted my life were **Humble, Grateful, Noble, and Faithful**. When I applied myself to learning not only what they meant but how to surrender my will to that wisdom, my processes, paradigms, and character changed. My entire life was elevated.

Virtues shape our world. From the inside out—when we commit to cultivating virtue and strength in our souls, we discover that everything outside is created by what we carry. This has been God's message to humanity from the beginning of time. He has informed us that His thoughts are higher, and we are invited to know them.

He says in Jeremiah 33:3, "Call to Me, and I will show you great and unsearchable things you do not know."

He also says in Proverbs 25:2, "It is to the glory of God to conceal a matter. It is to the glory of kings to search it out." His will was never to hide wisdom from us—but to hide it for us to search out and find. It's for the diligent, passionate, willing heart who will pursue the higher matters of life. God wants us to want what is precious so that we will treasure it.

What treasure is waiting for you? What wisdom is right there, hidden within today—waiting to be discovered? Here are some of the life-shaping thoughts I've gathered over decades of collecting wisdom about the four magic words.

Humble

Being humble—agreeing with God—changes our thinking patterns, and when thinking patterns change, so do behaviors and, ultimately, character. Yes, people can become entirely different human beings when humility has precedence in daily life.

Pace is one noticeable change. Humble people have an incredible ability to set a pace that produces the best possible outcome. The Bible says humility paces response. Humble people are slow to anger and speak. The pace of the humble creates a space to gather information and assess clarity and grace before conclusions are drawn and words are spoken. Influential leaders possess this superpower of humble pacing.

Humble people are rooted in confidence, which is far greater than pride. It's confidence granted by God, and it's unshakable. When we humble ourselves before the Lord, He exalts, lifts us, and honors us—in a way pride cannot duplicate. James 4:10 Pride has to be right to be secure. Humility doesn't—because humility knows we are all constantly students in life. Nothing is demeaning in the seat of learning. Don't be afraid of staying silent and waiting for wisdom from on high.

When we choose the gateway of humility and wait for God's wisdom, He gives it to us as promised. "Wisdom from on high is pure..." James 3:17. It will help us see and make the best possible choice—and help others as well.

Grateful

When we are grateful and live purposefully in that attitude, we feel different. Full. There's something about gratitude that allows us to feel complete, even when there are still needs in life. We can feel fully satisfied with what we already have, knowing God is still supplying, so there is nothing to fear. There is no fear of missing out. Gratitude has an underlying message: *I have enough now. I will have enough later. God will never cease to be good to me.*

Gratitude develops contentment within our souls. It heals our perspective. Instead of thinking we don't have enough—we see our hands full, and our hearts feel it, too. Godliness with contentment makes a person able to enjoy what's in their hand, heart, stomach, bank, or closet. See 1 Timothy 6:6-11

When we enjoy what we have, we are not lured into the consumerist sad song that tells us we don't have enough. Gratitude lets us savor the food on the fork, the clothes in the closet, the moments we have lived, and the ones we are in now.

When we are thankful, we see the people closest to us as gifts and cherish them. Gratitude makes people in every social class and economic condition see their blessings. It allows them to taste, sense, and enjoy the richness of life.

"Enter His gates with Thanksgiving." Psalm 100:4 There, in God's presence, is fullness of joy, pleasures to satisfy the soul, and favor that goes on forever. Psalm 16:11. But only the grateful will see it and receive it. Only those who calibrate their appetite with gratitude will have and enjoy life.

Noble

The heart attitude of nobility changes the thought patterns of all who embrace it. A person who has received their crown and the call as a child of God doesn't use it to lord over others 1 Peter 5:3. Instead, they use their exalted soul to lift others. The Father is known as "the lifter of my head," from David's description in Psalms 3:3. God sees us, not in our sins, but through the redeeming cross of Christ. When He sees us, He sees righteousness. This boggles the mind. We are kings and priests for the great calling God has planned. Revelation 5:10. And with this gift of dignity, we lift others.

When we see others struggling with anxiety or pride, humility slows our pace and allows us to see people the way the Father sees them. Next, gratitude reminds us of the path God walked us through—and that every person is being invited to that path.

Gratitude causes our full heart to run over with words of kindness and support—always ready to open the door for another to enter into grace. A noble heart moves through these virtues and believes in God's plan to bring peace and dignity to every person.

Don't be moved by what you see or hear from the one standing before you. Only be moved by the One who lives within you. A noble heart is an ambassador of peace—always ready to share a word with someone in need. Always ready to follow the Spirit —in silent kindness or words of hope.

Faithful

One of my favorite memories in the mentoring work is a golden phrase that emerged from a conversation with one of our clients. She was heartbroken, abused, and disillusioned with the idea of marriage. As we talked about her multiple relationships and the cloudy mess they created in her soul, I suggested she call a sabbatical from sex and invest in her mental and spiritual health to rebuild what broken relationships and insignificant sex had done in her life.

When I raised the topic of marriage and lifelong love, she scoffed, "Marriage is a fairy tale! It doesn't exist."

Her pain was speaking—and I knew it. Compassion welled up within me. I had made a statement that, in her world, meant nothing. It was as if healthy marriages didn't exist in her world, so I needed to translate it.

Marriage, in her eyes, was a concept that had been damaged by the example of people who perhaps failed to understand and live it out before her. What did she understand? Her fears, feelings, and the Media. The media, movies, music, and social media are the language of our generation.

So, I began to speak in media terms. "Have you ever heard of the series *Band of Brothers*? Or how about *Saving Private Ryan*?

The powerful message that flows through these movies is love and loyalty—not in the form of marriage, but they are the perfect example of what marriage could look like—if people took it seriously.

I posed this question to her:
"Everyone wants to be loved. Everyone wants loyalty, right?"
"Yes," she answered.

"Consider those movies—there is a great cost to loyalty. When we fight for each other, side by side—that's love. When we fight until we both win—that's loyalty."

"Who doesn't want that?"

"Everyone wants that," she responded.

"That's what marriage is supposed to look like. Just because you haven't seen it in real life doesn't mean there's not someone out there willing to go to war with and for you. That's what I'm suggesting."

To live with a faithful heart is just that. God ennobles us to be valiant soldiers and kings—ready to go to war for what's good and right. We don't fight against people—we fight for them.

The Bible says we do not war against flesh and blood but against spiritual entities that wage war against humanity. Ephesians 6:12 When we are faithful—our loyalty empowers us to bravely face these enemies, and through Christ—we win! Every time!

Faithfulness has grit. Galatians 5:6 tells us that faith is activated by love. That core of love reminds us of the truth; we are energized for this journey by a force that has no end. God. He pours this power into us through His Spirit. We stand in His love, live in His might, and by His grace, we become like Him—faithful.

Action Steps

1. **Reflect on the Four Virtues:** Spend time meditating on the virtues of humility, gratitude, nobility, and faithfulness. Consider how each can shape your attitudes and actions daily.

2. **Practice Seeing Others Through God's Eyes:** When encountering others, especially in challenging moments, intentionally choose to "see the gold" in them and respond with kindness and grace.

3. **Commit to Faithful Living:** Identify one area in your life where you can demonstrate greater faithfulness and loyalty—whether in relationships, work, or personal growth—and take concrete steps to embody that commitment.

Build You for Life

Odds are, you will work five days a week, eight hours a day, for the rest of your life. That's roughly 90,000 hours invested in someone else's business. How much time are you investing in building your life? Before you start doing the math or rolling your eyes in shame or frustration, here's the behavior of the average person:

The average person doesn't invest in exercise or reading regularly. Only 21% exercise daily. 14-44% depending on age, read daily. Interestingly, depending on the source, 44% pray daily.

The point I want to drive home here is this: your life is your business. Your body and mind are the workplace, and they make up the work culture within.

I hope that this book will be just the beginning of your journey—or a huge springboard on a path you're already traveling—in the process of healing and building the life you long to live. This is not a dress rehearsal. This is it!

The first step in the process is taking responsibility. That's a challenge in a culture that wants nothing to do with carrying anything heavy. Why? Because we are wired for strength! But we won't discover that strength until we start training it.

We only make gains when we do the work of strength training. The journey—from humility, through gratitude, accepting nobility as God intends it, and becoming a rock-solid person who can walk through any storm and remain loyal and faithful—that's making gains. Gains that make every other endeavor exponentially easier. Inner strength feeds all strength.

When you began the process of this book—because let's be honest, this is not a read, this is a process—you had things in mind that you wanted to see change. Some of these things may show signs of change already. Bigger matters will need more time committed to the process.

Whether you are working to unload the weight of serious trauma or the nagging fear of the future, the process is the same: Follow the steps encouraged throughout the book.

Quiet yourself. Pray. Gather wisdom from the Bible. Write down the inspirations that anchor you during prayer. Encourage yourself throughout the day—living with intentional focus and deliberate application.

Layer the care. This is something I tell my family when they are ill, in pain, or anxious. Don't just throw one dart of care at it and hope it does the trick. Layer the care. Do the same with building. Your life. Think of it as a brick building, one brick after the after, layer on layer. Shake off the "take a pill," *bippity-boppity-boo* mentality. This is layers of discipline, applied over time, to create the outcome you dream of. *Build You for Life* is a mindset—a commitment to build, one brick at a time.

Building and winning begin with wisdom.

Wisdom builds! It's a phrase I use often. Of course, it does so much more. Here's another mini motto that can be granted to this virtue: Wisdom wins! When we follow wisdom, we learn that it flows like a river—and ends up in the same place every time: victory. It's just like its twin: Love. Love and wisdom never fail. They always win.

When we make way for wisdom, building brick by brick with the insight gained through prayer, reading, and listening to wise people, our outcome is secure. We win!

Proverbs 24:6 says, *"For by wise guidance you can wage your war, and in abundance of counselors there is victory."*

The process you are implementing—through prayer, journaling, reading, and meditating on the Bible—is like gathering bricks for your cathedral of life. It's like gathering warriors around you before going into battle.

It's easy to read a book like this and think, *Yeah, it worked for them,* and then add your own conclusion of why it worked *for them* but might not work for you.

Here are a couple of thoughts I want to offer if you are skeptical about this process and whether it works for everyone:

First, it *does* work - for everyone who lives by it.

Wisdom is a spiritual force, not a lottery card. God used wisdom to create the universe, and again to redeem us when we chose to rebel against Him, not knowing it would condemn us to darkness. When we went our own way, wisdom started strategizing a new way. That's why Christ came to Earth, lived, served, died, and came back to life through the power of the Holy Spirit. He is the embodiment of love and wisdom.

Wisdom will always do exactly what God intends because wisdom, just like love, is the life force of God. It will give life, redeem life, heal, and build a life. Wisdom *will* work for you—

if you implement it consistently for the rest of your life. If that sounds too hard, let me remind you: you're going to do something for the rest of your life. You might as well do the right thing—and build a life of peace.

Be Willing to Go First

A very important point that must be made in any book about relationship restoration is this: **It takes two to tango.** My story reflects that truth. Both of us were at fault in those early years. We had baggage and ignorance to deal with. Whenever there is a problem in life, whether at home or at work, someone needs to address it. Going first doesn't make us a doormat or a champion. It makes us a change agent. It's not going to feel good. It's going to feel uncertain and painful. You will have to fight to be objective. Gather wisdom from wise people, from prayer and the Bible, and move forward. Resist thoughts of self-pity or glorification. Stay objective. Go first. Face the music and dance.

I was the first one dancing. That was a risk—a scary, uncertain risk. There was no guarantee my husband would change. Important to note: My husband was not abusive or unkind. He was simply unaware—unaware of what I needed, or how to care for me in a way that made me feel loved. He was unaware of the realm of emotional and relational intelligence, but he was ready to grow and learn to build his life. Thankfully, when I started down the path of love, I gained wisdom and understanding. That wisdom helped me react differently in moments of disappointment and frustration. I changed my modus operandi. He noticed and felt it—and that love welcomed him into the process of change. It gave him the space and safety to take risks of his own and learn how to love and believe for more.

It's scary to risk like that. It's terrifying to wonder if your efforts will be enough to save your family. If that sounds like your story, don't go this road alone! Make God your anchor. He's the only one who can truly hold your soul steady. He will pour so much love into your heart that the risk will feel smaller and softened. You'll have the spiritual energy to love—even when it feels one-sided. God's love will enable you to love unconditionally.

Word of Caution

This entire book is presented to you and assumes you will take responsibility for yourself and transform your reality. However, there will be individuals reading this who are in unsafe relationships. This book will not change someone else.

If you are in an abusive relationship, whether verbal, emotional, or physical, please hear this clearly: you need to find a safe place and get help. Look up local or national hotlines. Reach out. Start the conversation. Your safety matters. You are not alone. Take action. Get safe.

You can encourage others, inspire them with your kindness, but being loyal in love does not mean tolerating abuse. You can walk away from abuse and still be a loyal person. Loyalty means choosing to love at all times—if necessary, from a distance.

Commit and Build

For most of us, safety is not the issue. The real issue is ignorance—and sometimes laziness. But we can overcome those deadweight habits. We can learn a new way of living.

It will require a ceasefire: no more blame-shifting, no more excuses. Your life is worth the effort. This book is all about building *you*. You cannot build someone else—only yourself.

As we wrap up, I thought it would be fun to wrap up with phrases that inspired me over this journey. Some of them I coined to encourage myself. Others were gleaned from great hearts. I have no tattoos, but if I ever get one, these will be the phrases I choose from.

"There is grace for growth."
Don't try to make it happen in an instant. Growth takes time. You will enjoy the slow-growth process when you choose to have grace for yourself. Give yourself time to grow. There is grace for growth.

"Don't settle for being an expert when you could live as an explorer."
Every time you want to park and say, "good enough," stop yourself. Every time you want to assume you've seen it all and can draw conclusions—stop yourself! There is more to learn—about yourself, people, and most certainly, God. Humility keeps us in that state of openness so we can continually learn and grow. Don't settle for being an expert when you could live as an explorer!

"See the gold and call it out."
Though I didn't coin this one, I live by it. It was a game-changer in our marriage. It worked! And I'm the richer one for it. See the gold in yourself, your family, friends, and anyone you're called to care for. "See the gold and call it out."

"Whatever He tells you to do—do it."
This originates with Mary, not Nike. It was what she told those working at the wedding in Cana right before the first miracle of Christ. John 2:5. When we live a life guided by those listening prayers, God will provide.

He will guide our steps, providing wisdom to build a better life. There are still miracles waiting to happen. Follow Christ and… "Whatever He tells you to do—do it!"

Build You!
In Proverbs 31:17, it reads: *"She equips herself with strength (spiritual, mental, and physical fitness for her God-given tasks) and makes her arms strong."* There is one person responsible to build your life—Build You! There is gold in your soul and purpose on your path! Build You each day—for life—with the grace and wisdom of God.

Thanks for sharing this journey with me. I have one request: Share it. Share the book, but more than that—share the journey! We stir strength in each other. Encourage your family and friends. See the potential in them and call it out! Encourage them! Build You! Build others!

This entire book has been focused on inner healing - building you from the inside out. I invite you to join me in my next book, as we will explore the great purpose of our lives - bringing light and life to our world!

Build You—for life! I'm cheering you on!

Bibliography

Books

Eastman, P. D. *Are You My Mother?* New York: Random House, 1960.

Hamp, Bob. *Think Differently, Live Differently: Keys to a Life of Freedom.* Bedford, TX: House of Healing Ministries, 2010.

Hardy, Darren. *The Compound Effect.* New York: Hachette Book Group, 2010.

Leaf, Caroline. *Cleaning Up Your Mental Mess: 5 Simple, Scientifically Proven Steps to Reduce Anxiety, Stress, and Toxic Thinking.* Grand Rapids, MI: Baker Books, 2021.

———. *Who Switched Off My Brain? Controlling Toxic Thoughts and Emotions.* Dallas, TX: Switch On Your Brain International, 2009.

Oatman, Johnson, Jr. *Count Your Blessings.* Lyrics by Johnson Oatman Jr., music by Edwin O. Excell, 1897.

St. John of the Cross. *Dark Night of the Soul.* Translated by E. Allison Peers. New York: Image Books, 1990.

Wilkinson, Bruce. *The Prayer of Jabez: Breaking Through to the Blessed Life.* Sisters, OR: Multnomah Publishers, 2000.

Warren, Rick. *The Purpose Driven Life: What on Earth Am I Here For?* Grand Rapids, MI: Zondervan, 2002.

Bible Translations
The Amplified Bible. Grand Rapids, MI: Zondervan, 2015.
The Holy Bible: New International Version. Grand Rapids, MI: Zondervan, 2011.
The Holy Bible: New Living Translation. Carol Stream, IL: Tyndale House Publishers, 2015.

Articles & Online Sources
Catholic Culture. "Woman of the 14th Century: St. Catherine." Accessed August 2025. https://www.catholicculture.org.

Centers for Disease Control and Prevention (CDC). "Physical Activity Facts." Accessed August 2025. https://www.cdc.gov.

Gettysburg College. "One-Third of Your Life Is Spent at Work." Accessed August 2025. https://www.gettysburg.edu.

Pew Research Center. "Religious Beliefs and Practices." 2024. https://www.pewresearch.org.

Podcasts
Peterson, Jordan. "Mercy and Justice." Interview by Jocko Willink. *Jocko Podcast,* episode 112. 2018.

Films & Media
Band of Brothers. Directed by David Frankel and Tom Hanks. HBO, 2001.

Cinderella. Directed by Clyde Geronimi, Hamilton Luske, and Wilfred Jackson. Walt Disney Productions, 1950.

Madame Blueberry. Directed by Mike Nawrocki and Phil Vischer. Big Idea Productions, 1998.

Saving Private Ryan. Directed by Steven Spielberg. DreamWorks Pictures, 1998.

About the Author

Sandy Ohlman - Sandy has dedicated her life to serving individuals in times of crisis. Through her coaching, she emphasizes the power of daily disciplines—grounded in faith and carried into every area of life—through prayer, Scripture, and journaling. Connect with her on Instagram @build_you_for_life or at SandyOhlman.com.

www.ingramcontent.com/pod-product-compliance
Lightning Source LLC
Chambersburg PA
CBHW032032040426
42449CB00007B/860